LOST SOULS OF THE RIVER KWAI

LOST SOULS
OF THE
RIVER KWAI

by
BILL REED
with
MITCH PEEKE

Pen & Sword
MILITARY

First published in Great Britain in 2004
Reprinted in this format in 2009 by
Pen & Sword Military
An imprint of
Pen & Sword Books Ltd
47 Church Street
Barnsley
South Yorkshire
S70 2AS

ISBN 978 184884 199 4

A CIP catalogue record for this book is
available from the British Library

Typeset in 11\13 Sabon by
Phoenix Typesetting, Auldgirth, Dumfriesshire

Printed and bound in England
By CPI

Pen & Sword Books Ltd incorporates the Imprints of Pen & Sword Aviation,
Pen & Sword Family History, Pen & Sword Maritime, Pen & Sword Military,
Wharncliffe Local History,
Pen & Sword Select, Pen & Sword Military Classics, Leo Cooper,
Remember When, Seaforth Publishing and Frontline Publishing

For a complete list of Pen & Sword titles please contact
PEN & SWORD BOOKS LIMITED
47 Church Street, Barnsley, South Yorkshire, S70 2AS, England
E-mail: enquiries@pen-and-sword.co.uk
Website: www.pen-and-sword.co.uk

We would like to dedicate this book to:

The memory of all those who suffered the nightmares but did not survive them, to all those who are still suffering them, and to all ex-prisoners' wives, who live them with us.

Bill

The memory of 'Diddy' my late paternal grandfather, who suffered those same nightmares in silence, for far too long. Also, to the memory of his son Jim, my late father.

Mitch

The memory of Ivy Mary Harris and Walter Byron Slater; my beloved sister and my uncle respectively, both whom died on the night of 9-10 April 1941 when enemy bombs fell on the family home, the Harbourne Home and Dispensary for Animals. I lost a great part of my life that night.

Beryl Martha Harris Reed

CONTENTS

FOREWORD

by Colonel T. L. May

I belong to a very fortunate generation – too young to have had to serve in the Second World War, but old enough to have had the relatively pleasant experience of National Service followed by many enjoyable years in the Territorial Army, including peacetime command of the Queen's Own Oxfordshire Hussars Battery of 299 Field Regiment, Royal Artillery.

A few years ago now, the last of the officers who had served in the Oxfordshire Yeomanry (QOOH) during the Second World War in 'field rank' had died, and I was subsequently asked to become President of the Regimental Association. By that time, I had met a number of our wartime veterans – though I hadn't met Bill Reed at that point – and was conscious of them being a very special group of people. I felt that they deserved someone very much more special than me as their figurehead and it was only after being persuaded that my extra life expectancy would be helpful in looking after their welfare interests, that I was persuaded to accept the Presidency of the Association.

The Old Comrades that are still with us in 2003 are 'survivors' in many senses of that word. I have come to know them as the people they are now, knowing only in outline, if at all, the details of their wartime experience and subsequent history. The fact is though, that the special quality of these men shines through whenever I meet them on regimental or other occasions. They seem to me to be people to whom self-reliance is second nature. They would prefer not to ask for help for themselves but invariably seek to give it, where needed, to others. They know who they are and are proud of it (but never, ever, arrogant). They, compared with many other elderly, seem to have discovered some secret of life unknown to most of us. I think it is not too much to say that, allowing for physical distress, they are happy in a way that few younger people seem able to discover.

Having now met Bill Reed and read his story, I can begin to understand a little better where that 'special' quality of our veterans comes from and how those survivors can have discovered a kind of happiness apparently denied to many of us today.

The story related in this book is partly of desperate, bumbling military incompetence by apparently craven commanders, succeeded after the conflict, by the manifest wish of the 'powers-that-be' to keep it from the public. It is partly about the gross inhumanity, not to be excused by cultural background, of a particular group of men at war when given responsibility for prisoners. It is very much about the ways in which sheer courage, coupled with ingenuity and a sometimes-necessary form of downright bloody-mindedness, can enable a group of captive comrades, supporting each other, to survive sustained privation and cruelty. Perhaps more significantly and positively, for all our sakes, it is about the ability of some to live through such treatment and despite it, subsequently to eventually live full, useful and contented lives.

Having suffered as they undoubtedly did, following what it is difficult not to see even now as a gross betrayal by their commanders, it must have been very hard for Bill and his comrades to take the insult implied by the authorities intention to 'forget' the whole thing. In a few years from now, all the eyewitnesses like Bill will have gone, and the authorities may finally achieve the obfuscation they've sought all along.

It is this aspect particularly, that makes Bill Reed's story of the 'other ranks' experience so relevant and valid at this time. Bill continues to suffer severe physical effects from his treatment at the hands of his captors. However, his memory and his ability to articulate, remain vivid. His story has already been, and will continue to be, wholly corroborated by his surviving comrades.

x

Fortunately, Bill has found in Mitch Peeke precisely the right person to put his important and revealing recollections into a book. Their synergy results in a story that resonates with truth that deserves to be told and will be very difficult to stop reading once started.

T. L. M.
May, 2003.

GLOSSARY

The more commonly used 'Japlish' words.

Bango	Number/Sound off
Benjo	Toilet
Bugairo	Japanese insult/curse
Dame dana	It's bad/ no good
Gunsho	Japanese Warrant Officer
Ichi,	One
Ni,	Two
San,	Three
Shi,	Four
Go	Five
Kempie	Military policeman (From 'kempeitai')
Leggies	Leftover food
Me Bioke	I'm sick/ill
Meishi	Eat
Nai	No
Nando?	What's going on?
No-good house	Punishment cell
Speedo!	Be quick/Hurry up!
Speedo-Benjo	Dysentery attack
Tenko	Roll call
Yasumi	Rest

AUTHOR'S INTRODUCTION

This book is not intended to provide entertaining reading and frankly, I make no apology for that. Having said that, there are more than a few light moments, but the main subject is far from comedic. This book is the story of what happened to one British soldier, Bill Reed, and how that experience has affected the rest of his life.

Bill Reed was just one man among the many thousands of men who were captured by the Imperial Japanese Army during what has become known as 'the forgotten war', the war fought in the Far East during the Second World War. Cut off, lacking air and sea support and with no prospect of the arrival of reinforcements, the 130,000 British troops in Singapore were ordered by their Commander-in-Chief, General Percival, to lay down their arms and surrender to the advancing Japanese Army of just 35,000 men on 15 February 1942.

The surrendering British troops were expecting nothing less than the treatment due to them as prisoners of war, under the terms of the Geneva Convention. The Japanese Army however, had no intention of observing such rules. The Japanese code of 'Bushido' had no place for surrender; it simply wasn't an option that Japanese troops ever considered. From the moment he entered training camp as a raw recruit, the Japanese soldier was taught that he either fought and won, or died gloriously for his Emperor in the attempt; 'Banzai'! To the Japanese, any soldier, enemy or otherwise, who surrendered, was simply sub-human, a coward even, and would be treated as such.

My late paternal grandfather, whom we always called 'Diddy'

due to his being the shortest member of the family, was a prisoner of the Japanese. He had been a serving London fireman during the first two years of the war and if there was one thing Diddy enjoyed, it was driving. Piloting a bright red Dennis fire engine, bell ringing, through London's blacked out, bomb-damaged streets on his way to yet another 'shout' during the Blitz of 1940, suited him down to the ground. In fact, in later years he used to drive his Morris Oxford saloon car in much the same manner, never using the clutch, as the Dennis fire engine had what was commonly referred to as a 'crash-change' gearbox. Diddy therefore opined that a clutch pedal was simply a luxury item fitted solely for use by lazy drivers. It was a good job that Morris cars had a strong gearbox!

When the Blitz ended early in 1941, Diddy volunteered his considerable driving experience to the Royal Air Force, who accepted him. Because of his experience he, like Bill, was a Driver IC. Posted to Burma, he was subsequently captured by the Japanese and put to work on the infamous Burma-Thailand railway, 'The Railway of Death', where it was later said that one British or Commonwealth prisoner had died for every sleeper that was laid.

It is only with the writing of Bill's story that I have come to understand something of the ordeal that my late grandfather went through, for he never spoke of it to his grandchildren. In fact, he never said much about it to his own children, but his wife Mary had some idea, for she lived the nightmare with him until the day she died. It is a nightmare that few people today can even begin to understand, as those who survived were ordered by the military authorities not to talk about it at the time.

The Diddy who came home from the war was no longer medically fit to return to the Fire Brigade, so he worked on the docks instead. But he was a very different man from the out-going, cheeky-monkey-faced ex-fireman who'd joined the RAF. Sadly, I only knew him as a seemingly aloof, cold, withdrawn and somewhat hard man, with a litany of medical problems, who sometimes smiled but rarely laughed.

Such too, is the background to Bill Reed's war. A war that physically started on 3 September 1939 and ended only after he had spent a gruelling three and a half years as a prisoner of the Japanese. However, it is very much a war that mentally, Bill, like so many others, is still fighting. The story in this book is Bill's nightmare – the nightmare that never goes away – but it is a nightmare that is destined to haunt all those who were forced to endure it, to the last.

Mitch Peeke,
Kent, October 2002.

LOST SOULS
OF THE
RIVER KWAI

Chapter One

OVER THE BRINK

On the morning of Sunday, 3 September 1939, an air of quiet foreboding prevailed over the entire British Isles. Just after 11 o'clock that morning, people from all walks of life stopped whatever they were doing, switched on their wirelesses and allowed the sets to warm up. The British Prime Minister, Neville Chamberlain, was due to address the nation at 11:15 a.m.

People all over the country, old and young, gathered around their wireless sets in subdued silence. People like sixteen-year old Beryl Harris, sitting with the rest of her family in the dining room of their home in Birmingham, and eighteen-year old Bill Reed, an apprentice stonemason and builder, in the garden of a friend's house in the village of Radway in Warwickshire, all listened intently as the sombre-toned voice of a heavy-hearted Neville Chamberlain, made the following announcement over the crackling airwaves of the BBC Home Service:

This morning, the British Ambassador in Berlin handed the German government a final note; stating that unless we heard from them, by eleven o'clock, that they were prepared at once to withdraw their troops from Poland, a state of war would exist between us. I have to tell you now, that no such undertaking has been received, and that consequently, this country is at war with Germany. It is a sad day for all of us. Every aim for which I have worked, everything I had hoped for, all the principles in which I believed, have fallen down in ruin. I hope to live long enough to see the day when Hitlerism will be destroyed, and a free Europe will exist again. For it is evil things that we shall be fighting against: Brute force, bad faith, injustice, oppression and

1

persecution; and against these, I am certain that the right will prevail.

Reactions to Chamberlain's momentous speech were mixed, but most were stunned by what they had heard. Those who could still recall the horrors of the last war angrily thought 'No! Not again!' Only twenty-one years had passed since the end of the Great War; now it suddenly seemed as though the overwhelming sacrifice made by the generation of 1914 had been wholly in vain.

For Beryl Harris, it was with shocked disbelief that she realized that the unthinkable had actually just happened. All the fervent hopes of what Chamberlain had once called 'peace in our time' had just been shattered by the renewed blast of war.

For Bill Reed, sitting in his friend's garden, it meant the final confirmation of his months-old belief that another war with Germany was inevitable. It was this conviction, plus the rather natty recruiting posters he had seen, that had compelled him to join the reserves, the Territorial Army, some months previously. On hearing the conclusion of the Prime Minister's speech, he left his friend's house and made his way immediately to the barracks of his unit; 252 battery of the 63 Anti-Tank Regiment, the Oxfordshire Yeomanry, at Banbury. Bill's war had begun.

During peacetime training, the Oxfordshires had shared their equipment with a neighbouring regiment, the Worcestershires. The equipment was divided equally between the two regiments. The Monday following the declaration of war, the colonels from both regiments met, and in one of those great moments in military history, they tossed a coin to see who got the full complement of equipment. The Oxfordshires lost. Having won the toss, the Worcestershires packed up the equipment and left immediately to join the British Expeditionary Force (BEF), that contingent of the British army that was sent to France to stem the expected German invasion. It was one of those moments when 'there but for the grace of God, go I' for although the men of the Oxfordshires were initially somewhat disappointed, they were later quite relieved to have been left behind. Not many of the Worcestershires survived the German onslaught when it came. The Oxfordshires were soon posted to nearby RAF Bicester, to guard the aerodrome.

It wasn't very long after the declaration of war that terrorist activity by the Irish Republican Army (IRA) was resumed. There had been a number of pillar-box bombings on the UK mainland by that organization, and Bill and his comrades had been warned to be especially vigilant because of this renewed terrorist activity. Added to that was the presumed threat from 'Fifth-Columnists' who were said to be everywhere. It was against this background that Bill came to fire his first shots in anger one moonlit night, while on guard duty outside the main hangar at RAF Bicester.

On the twelve till two stint, Bill and 'Nabber' Atkins saw some shadows flitting about behind some large piles of bricks. The bricks had been piled up for the construction of pillboxes around the perimeter of the airfield, which at that time wasn't properly fenced, and the piles of bricks were about sixty-five yards or so away from Bill and Nabber. They had been quietly talking when they heard some strange, muffled grunting noises coming from the vicinity of the brick piles. Suddenly, Bill saw something moving behind the bricks as well.

Bill had finished as the runner-up in the regimental shooting championships recently, so it was decided that he should creep forward whilst Nabber issued the challenge. 'Halt! Who goes there?' shouted Nabber, raising his rifle as Bill crept forward. There was no response to Nabber's challenge apart from more muffled noises. 'Halt! Who goes there? Friend or foe?' challenged an increasingly alarmed Nabber. Still the only response was more shadowy movements from behind the bricks. Bill had now quietly advanced by about half the distance. 'Halt or I fire!' shouted Nabber nervously. Still no verbal response, but Bill could now see that there was definitely more than one of them, whoever they were, behind the bricks.

A sudden movement from behind the nearest pile of bricks brought instant reaction from Bill. He stood up and let off five rounds of rapid fire, shouting to Nabber to call out the guard. All hell broke loose. As the sounds of the shots he'd fired died away, Bill could just discern some faint moaning from behind the brick piles, so he knew he'd hit someone.

Within seconds it seemed, the rest of the guard arrived, summoned by Nabber's frantic blowing of his guard's whistle. About twenty of them then cautiously advanced with rifles at the ready. The sight that met Bill's eyes has stayed with him to this day, for there in the moonlight, behind the bricks, lay three very dead 'terrorist' cows!

Bill's comrades pulled his leg about cattle-killing for quite a while after that episode. To compound his embarrassment and further the delight of Bill's comrades, the *News of the World* ran an 'in depth' story about the bovine invasion of an aerodrome 'somewhere in England' that had been successfully repulsed by the base's staunch defenders. The 'enemy' had suffered heavy casualties whilst the defenders had suffered none. With such sterling troops guarding our shores, the article assured its readers, any invading German would know exactly what to expect! To make matters worse, the Army held an inquiry into the incident and Bill was put on a charge, but the matter was quietly dropped eventually.

In January of 1940, 252 Battery was re-equipped and moved to the grounds of Woodley House in Kineton, Warwickshire. Due to the extensive grounds, the Army had the use of Woodley for training purposes and 252 Battery was sent there for advanced training.

Since 1929, Woodley House had been the home of John Verney, the twentieth Lord Willoughby de Broke, and his wife Rachel, but they were now at RAF Tangmere in Sussex where John Willoughby was in command of a fighter squadron, 605 Auxiliary Squadron, RAF. He later went on to become Group Controller at 11 Group, RAF Fighter Command, which bore the brunt of the Battle of Britain. Willoughby's job as a fighter controller was to guide the RAF's Spitfire and Hurricane fighters to a successful interception of the incoming German air raids, a job he performed with a remarkable calmness and proficiency.

At Woodley House, about thirty members of the 1st Militia joined 252 Battery. The 1st Militia were the first batch of men to be conscripted to the armed forces. They were all aged twenty-one. Among this new intake was a man named Cyril Thompson.

Cyril had already served in the army and had been attached to the Palestine Police. His experience made him a first class drill instructor hence he was given the obvious nickname 'Squad'. He and Bill instantly became friends as the two shared a similar outlook on life and humour. By this time, Gunner Bill Reed had also passed the Army's driving tests and was now promoted to Driver IC. (Driver in Charge.)

The winter of 1939–40 was a harsh one with heavy snowfalls. One task that frequently fell to the troops billeted at Woodley House was the digging out of snow-bound trains. The Oxford main line was nearby and many were the calls to turn out at all hours of the day and night to labour on the railway. This was not exactly Bill's idea of a war, yet it was a strange precursor of what was to come.

Part of the advanced training programme at Woodley House involved nocturnal orienteering exercises. Six or eight men led by an NCO were driven some seven miles distance from the camp in a lorry, dropped off in the middle of nowhere and told to make their way back to Woodley House using the map and compass provided. Bill's group quickly proved to be remarkably proficient at this exercise, seemingly returning to camp in record time.

Initially, their Troop Officer, Lieutenant Tim Windsor, thought he had a body of outstanding men in his Troop, and rewarded Bill's group with packets of cigarettes or some other such luxury item. As the exercises progressed though, Lieutenant Windsor quickly began to have his suspicions about the orienteering prowess of his men. He'd noticed that it only ever seemed to be the group that had Driver Bill Reed leading it that made it back to camp first. Windsor had changed the composition of the groups on various nights and the common denominator to the successful group had always been Driver Reed.

One night, while Bill was not within earshot, Lieutenant Windsor asked the rest of the men in 252 Battery a question: 'Can anyone enlighten me as to why Reed's group is always the first back?' After some pensive seconds, during which a good few soldiers' feet had been nervously shuffled, Bombardier 'Waffy' Grant confessed that Bill lived in Radway before the war. All suddenly became clear to Windsor; the village of Radway was approximately three miles as the crow flies from Woodley House. Before the war, Bill and his friends had set up their own 'explorer's club', going for long walks covering many miles of the surrounding countryside. Consequently he literally knew the area like the back of his hand. Upon making this startling discovery, Lieutenant Windsor promptly took Bill off the orienteering exercises and assigned him to guard duty instead. The time taken by the groups to complete these night exercises suddenly ceased to be quite so impressive!

In May 1940, Operation Dynamo began. The beleaguered BEF and surviving Allied soldiers had to be hurriedly evacuated from the beaches of Dunkirk. The unstoppable German blitzkrieg had blasted through the Low Countries and France, sweeping all before it into a pocket around Dunkirk. Now, as the remains of the BEF, harried by the German Luftwaffe, were being ferried home across the channel in an armada of little ships, it seemed highly likely that a German invasion of England was imminent.

The War Emergency Act was implemented alongside an even stricter enforcement of the Defence of the Realm Act. All sorts of anti-invasion measures were put into place. Road signs were removed, the Local Defence Volunteers, which changed its name to the Home Guard in July 1940, was formed, anti-glider poles were erected and concealed trenches were dug across open fields. Barbed wire and checkpoints sprang up everywhere and the ARP (Air Raid Precautions) wardens enforced a strict blackout at night. People later said that the blackout injured almost as many people as German bombs did!

Bill's regiment was hurriedly moved south to meet the expected invasion and 252 Battery found itself stationed at Fort Fareham, Cosham, near the naval base at Portsmouth. It was a time of anxiety, for nobody knew what to expect. Invasion watch was a time of seemingly endless guard duty for Bill and his comrades.

The well-intentioned anti-invasion obstacles such as

concertinas of dannet wire and hidden trenches became a constant hazard to the guarding troops during the night blackout. As a result, Bill and his comrades developed an ingenious method of marking these hazards so that they didn't become the unwitting victims of the traps.

The area around the camp was literally alive with glow-worms and at dusk, the sentries used to put about five of these glow-worms into a half-open matchbox and set it down next to the obstacles on their round. From a distance, these 'markers' couldn't be seen, but as the patrolling sentries got to within about ten feet or so, they'd see this little glowing marker and know to take extra care where they trod. For some reason best known to them, the glow-worms apparently never wriggled out of the matchbox, so they made perfect markers. The relief sentries used to let all of the glow-worms go at dawn and collect the matchboxes ready for the next night.

As the threat of invasion diminished and the RAF fighter pilots fought the Battle of Britain overhead, Bill's regiment was posted to Newbury in Berkshire, to Benham Park. The summer of 1940 was a glorious one, so the regiment camped at Benham under canvas.

Shortly after their arrival, the regiment was equipped with a consignment of 500cc BSA and Norton motorcycles. Some were solo machines and some were motorcycle and sidecar machine-gun outfits. The object was to train the regiment in mechanized warfare. The BEF's experiences in France had showed the value of the highly mobile units of the German Army, and the Germans had used their excellent 750cc BMW motorcycles very effectively on the Continent.

As they grew more proficient in the skills needed to handle the motorcycles, an idea began to take shape in some of the soldiers' minds. All around Benham Park was a gravel track, which ended just past a large lake with a low parapet wall protecting it. An ideal racetrack! The timing for the proposed race was crucial; there could be no officers around. Sundays seemed to offer the best chance.

Ever one for a dare, Bill entered the sidecar event on a 500cc

BSA outfit. The 'chair-man' was his good friend Cyril 'Squad' Thompson. As the race got under way, Bill and Squad took an early lead, but the rest of the field were maintaining the pressure and their lead was tenuous. However, Bill's over-confidence caused him to lose control of the outfit within sight of the finish line. Applying too much throttle on the loose gravel surface, he put the outfit into a slide on a bend by the lake. Bill over-corrected, applied the brakes and the slide turned into a desperate skid, which saw the outfit tear straight through the low parapet wall and plunge into the lake.

Fortunately for Bill and Squad, the point they entered the lake was not much more than two feet deep with a muddy bottom. The outfit came to rest upright in a spectacular cloud of spray, with water vapour steaming off the hot engine and the bike's electrics very much the worse for being immersed. Bill was still more or less in the saddle, though somewhat further forward than was usual, whilst Squad found that he was crammed as far forward as it was possible to be in a military sidecar half-full with water.

As the sergeant in charge of the Motor Transport section was in on the race, the outfit was hastily retrieved from the lake, taken to the workshop and quickly stripped down for repair. All Bill and Squad had to do was to hide all the loose masonry their passage through the wall had created, change their uniforms (and dry the wet ones out unobtrusively) then pretend that their bruises didn't hurt at all whilst suffering the inevitable round of whispered 'motorpike and sidecarp' or 'U-bike' jokes from those in the know!

Shortly after the motorcycle incident, the regiment received another posting. This time it was to Millbrook near Lisburn in Northern Ireland. The object of the posting was for more in-tensive training in preparation for a proposed future invasion of Norway. They were based at Lisburn and Port Stewart alternately for the next fourteen months and the schedule of extensive manoeuvres left little time for skylarking.

In September 1941, Bill, Squad and eight others, volunteered to transfer to 251 Battery in order to form a new regiment; the 85

Anti-Tank Regiment, Royal Artillery. Their ever-popular Troop Officer, Lieutenant Windsor later told them that if he'd known in advance that they were volunteering, he'd have gone with them. Lieutenant Windsor subsequently joined the Airborne Division and trained as a glider pilot. Sadly, he was later killed in action during the assault landings at Arnhem, in 1944.

The men who were to form the 85 Anti-Tank Regiment were immediately ordered back to Britain. You can imagine their surprise when they found themselves posted to Butlin's holiday camp at Clacton! There, they were equipped with brand new kit, new lorries and new motorcycles. As all the lorries had an unusually high ground clearance and all of the vehicles were painted in a sort of sand-colour, there were no prizes for guessing that they were off to fight in the desert somewhere. The only questions were, when and where?

The answers were not long in coming. The new regiment, now called somewhat long-windedly 251 Battery, Oxfordshire Yeomanry, 85 Anti-Tank Regiment of the Royal Artillery, was posted to Basra in the Persian Gulf. It was, as Bill says, a bloody long way and a bloody long name! There wasn't much they could do about the distance to the Persian Gulf, but they decided that henceforth, they would simply be known as the 85th Anti-Tank Regiment, Royal Artillery.

Once the newly formed regiment was given its orders, embarkation leave was granted. Bill and his troop however, were assigned the task of transporting the regiment's kit and equipment to the docks at Glasgow. The regiment was embarked on board a former P&O passenger liner, the SS *Narkunda*.

The ship sailed in a convoy escorted by HMS *Royal Sovereign* and attendant corvettes, in mid-October, bound for Durban, South Africa. The convoy was routed north practically to Iceland, and then far out into the North Atlantic to avoid the areas most frequented by German U-boats, before finally making its turn onto the long southward leg of its journey to Durban. Despite this precaution, the convoy was attacked by U-boats several times. The nights were the worst, as Bill recalled. One minute all would be quiet then suddenly would come the sound of depth-charges exploding as the escorts engaged a U-boat. It was quite nerve-racking for those aboard the troopships and the other merchantmen, but each time the U-boats attacked, the escorting warships successfully kept the wolf packs at bay. This convoy was the most heavily protected outbound convoy of the war so far, and it paid off.

It was while they were at sea that they heard of the Japanese attack on the American Pacific Fleet at Pearl Harbor on Sunday, 7 December. Though they did not know it yet, what President Roosevelt called 'a date that will live in infamy' would have a remarkable bearing on the lives of all the troops in that convoy.

The convoy arrived safely in Durban after a brief stop at Freetown, on 22 December 1941. During the short time that they were there, Bill, Squad Thompson and two others found themselves attached to the Military Police. With so many servicemen allowed shore leave after the lengthy voyage from England, it was inevitable that their pent-up spirits would find a release ashore. Rickshaw races abounded, causing some minor injuries, but by far the most frequent duties performed by the Military Police squads were bar and brothel clearance operations. In either case, the servicemen were reluctant to leave the premises and usually had to be forcibly removed by the Redcaps.

Just two scant days after their arrival in Durban however, an urgent signal was received *en clair* from the *Royal Sovereign*. It read:

SS. NARKUNDA: HAVE YOU THE NECESSARY CHARTS FOR PASSAGE TO SINGAPORE VIA SUNDRA AND BANKA STRAITS?

The answer was in the affirmative, which effectively sealed the fates of the men of the 85 Anti-Tank Regiment. All shore leave was cancelled and as soon as everybody was accounted for, *Narkunda* set sail on Christmas Eve. She proceeded unescorted across the Indian Ocean.

The urgency was due to the fact that Japanese forces had landed in Malaya the day after the attack on Pearl Harbor. On 10 December, the Royal Navy lost two capital ships, HMS *Repulse* and HMS *Prince of Wales* in action off Malaya and the

Japanese raided Penang on 11 December followed by Burma the next day. The Japanese seemed to have learned something about the waging of 'lightning war' from their German allies. The situation was so grave that Bill's convoy had been diverted from its original destination and sent to Singapore in the hopes of stopping the Japanese onslaught.

Narkunda made a one-day stopover at the Maldives to allow the ship carrying the regiment's equipment and kit to catch up. Shore leave was not permitted, but up on deck, leaning against the rail, Bill could not help but marvel at the sheer beauty of the Maldives with their white sand beaches and abundance of palm trees. It was the last friendly land that Bill would see for the next three and a half years, and he would soon come to view palm trees in a totally different light.

Chapter Two

BAPTISM OF FIRE

Singapore: Gateway to the Pacific. Half of the world's rubber came from Malaya at that time and a third of the world's tin. The British Empire needed these precious commodities and in 1921, the British decided to fortify the island and to build a huge naval base there. The fleet of mighty Royal Navy warships that was to occupy this base would not in fact reside there. It would be sent from England to Singapore if ever it were needed. What was then referred to as 'the period of relief' was set as being seventy days. In other words, the Royal Navy was never more than seventy days sailing from Singapore; an apparently acceptable situation.

In 1923, British military planners agreed that there was absolutely no possibility of an attack being made upon Singapore from a northerly direction. Infantry, it was thought, would find the dense mangrove swamps and the jungle of Malaya totally impassable. The most likely prospect was a sea-borne invasion.

Three years later, Winston Churchill, who had been instrumental in the earlier decision to fortify the island of Singapore, was evidently having second thoughts about it. He told the Committee for Imperial Defence that if he'd known then the financial burden such a project would place on Britain, he would never have agreed to it. Although the British wanted the rubber and tin, they didn't want to spend any money on protecting their interests, unless they really had to.

In 1936, the then General Officer Commanding Singapore, General Dobbie, stated that an attack on Singapore from the north was precisely what he feared. He also stated that the jungle to the north and north-west was not, in fact, impenetrable. Nobody believed him. Singapore's defences had, in any case, largely been built to cover every direction except the north, in line with the earlier thinking concerning an attack largely from the sea.

In September 1940, Churchill, by then Prime Minister, stated that Singapore's defence rested upon the fleet. The Middle East Fleet could always be sent to Singapore at short notice and it was, in his view, extremely unlikely that the Japanese would gamble by attacking Singapore's fortified defences. The Japanese were inclined to agree with him on that point. Even the Air Officer Commanding Singapore decided that it would be best not to send Hurricanes and Spitfires to bolster Singapore's air defences. In his opinion, Brewster Buffalo fighters were more than adequate for Malaya. Sadly, events were to prove the AOC Singapore and Winston Churchill very wrong and General Dobbie entirely correct.

In October of 1940, the powers that be decided that Malaya needed no more than 556 aircraft. Strangely enough, the Japanese had reached almost the same conclusion. They committed 534 aircraft to their offensive. Unfortunately for the British, the Japanese sent 534 of their best and most modern aircraft, completely outclassing the obsolete Brewster Buffalo and Vickers Wildebeest types with which the RAF tried to defend Singapore. Given the fortifications, the Japanese attack on Singapore, when it came, was not from the sea. One cannot help but compare the situation in Singapore late in 1941, with that of the fabled Maginot Line in France in 1940.

The SS *Narkunda* steamed slowly into Singapore on 13 January 1942. Everybody was on deck, eagerly awaiting the first glimpse of this tropical land. But their welcome was not at all what they expected. The 'reception committee' took the form of some twenty Japanese fighter-bombers, bombing and strafing the harbour.

The first Bill realized of this was as the man next to him pointed at the water and said to look at the splashes the fish were making. As Bill looked, he saw a twin line of splashes raking the water near the ship and realized in an instant that far from being fish, the splashes were being made by bullets! Everyone literally hit the deck as a Japanese Zero fighter roared low over the ship and sped out to sea. Fortunately for them, though they hadn't realized it at that point, the ship had taken evasive action and spoiled the Japanese pilot's aim. 'Welcome to Singapore' said someone sardonically, as the Japanese planes departed.

When *Narkunda* finally docked, the troops were disembarked and moved straight to an old Indian Army barracks called Birdwood Camp, near Changi. Once settled in, they were given twelve hours leave, from 18:00 to 06:00, during which they were free to sample the delights of Singapore.

Bill and Squad Thompson, two of their friends, Jackie Boyce and Frank Steadman, and one other whose name Bill cannot now recall, duly went into Singapore City for a night out. The first thing they did was to buy a book of tickets costing $1.00 to go taxi-dancing. They went into the Happy World nightclub where each dance cost ten cents. The girls were mostly Thai or Malay and they were renowned for their stunning appearance. As the dance finished they would always ask the soldiers for an extra thirty cents to 'buy mama a coffee'. It was also made crystal clear that there were 'other services' available, not just dancing.

Having sampled some of the delights of the Happy World and the Wide World nightclubs, Bill and his mates also went 'window-shopping' along Lavender Road. (For those readers unfamiliar with this thoroughfare, Canal Street, Amsterdam is equally famed!)

It was in the early hours of the morning that the five friends decided it was time to head back to camp and sought to find a taxi. Unbeknown to the five, the taxis were not permitted beyond the city limits after midnight. Nobody had told the soldiers of this civilian curfew. As far as they were aware, they had until 06:00 to return to Birdwood Barracks, some fifteen miles away.

They soon found a taxi and all five of them piled into it, telling the driver to take them to Birdwood Camp. Tapping his watch, the taxi driver said 'No! City limits. Me go only city limits.' Bill thought the driver was being unnecessarily awkward for some reason and insisted that they be taken to the barracks. 'No! City limits!' said the driver. Bill was now angry. 'Then you stay here' Bill said, 'and we'll take the taxi'! With that, Bill got out of the cab, pulled the taxi driver out from behind the wheel and took his place. Bill then drove the now stolen taxi away with his four friends in the back, toward Birdwood Camp.

Whether the taxi driver reported the theft of his cab or not, Bill doesn't know, but they'd only travelled about ten miles when they encountered a roadblock manned by the Redcaps, the military police. Bill slammed the brakes on and steered the taxi off the road, straight into a ditch. Nobody needed telling that it would be a good idea to make themselves scarce and all five of them scrambled out of the cab to hide in the undergrowth. Unfortunately for them, the Redcaps quickly caught Jackie Boyce, who surrendered his paybook to the military policeman who had hold of him.

The next thing the four remaining fugitives heard was the 'sergeant majorish' tone of the Redcaps' patrol officer shouting: 'Right, you can all come out now! We've got Boyce and we know that you're all from the 85 Anti-Tank. Show yourselves!'

There wasn't much else they could do. The remaining four all came out of hiding and were promptly arrested. They were held in a tent while the Redcaps made further enquiries about the taxi, checked the men's identities and telephoned Birdwood Camp. After about two hours or so, an officer from Birdwood arrived to take charge of the miscreants and escort them back to camp.

At 09:00 the next morning, all five men were waiting outside the tent of their commanding officer, Colonel Lardener-Clarke. Inside the tent, the colonel in charge of the military police was apprising Colonel Lardener-Clarke of what had taken place the night before. After a heavy discussion, the Redcap colonel emerged from the tent, gave the five waiting men a doubtful look and departed. The five were then marched into Colonel Lardener-Clarke's presence.

Their Colonel was extremely stern-faced as he delivered what Bill described as 'a right royal rocket' to the five miscreants.

Coming to the end of his admonishing of the men, Colonel Lardener-Clarke said:

> However, the Redcap colonel and I have decided that no further action will be taken in this matter. The only reason for this is the fact that we are going into action tomorrow morning and you five blackguards just might get killed and save us both the trouble! Therefore, you will hear no more about it. Dismiss!

As the five put their hats back on and saluted, the Colonel added; 'Good luck anyway, men.' The five were promptly marched out, leaving their Colonel to shake his head and wonder at them.

Two hours after Bill and his cohorts had been 'lectured', the 85 Anti-Tank Regiment, which had spent fourteen months training for an invasion of Norway and then been equipped for war in the desert, was hurriedly attached to the 11 Indian Brigade, and moved some fifty miles north of Birdwood Camp to Jahore Baru, in order to fight a jungle war in Malaya.

Next morning found them in action in a rubber plantation just north of the Sultan of Jahore's palace, trying to delay the advancing Japanese by denying them use of the main road. As Bill was a Driver IC, one of his jobs was to drive the Troop Officer, Lieutenant Carpenter, around while they reconnoitred new gun positions. They were fighting a desperate rearguard action already. The 11 Indian Brigade was trying to hold a line to allow British and Empire troops to withdraw.

The fighting was confused, right from the start, with sporadic rifle and artillery fire interspersed with strafing by Japanese fighter aircraft. The surrounding terrain was a mixture of jungle and mangrove swamps, both presumed by the British commanders to be impenetrable. At first, it seemed to the men that their commanders might be correct in that presumption, as the first encounter that Bill had with the Japanese Army was almost laughable. They were dug in beside a road when about thirty or forty Japanese soldiers came along the road on bicycles. The hidden British troops heard them before they saw them. The Japanese soldiers appeared to be riding along without a care and for the whole world to see. Rather like a cycle club outing!

16

They obviously hadn't seen the British soldiers, who watched them as them as they filled their sights.

The men of Bill's regiment waited until the Japanese soldiers were almost on top of them and then opened up with everything they had. In a matter of seconds the Japanese were all accounted for. Such 'easy meat' was a rarity though, as Bill and his colleagues were later to discover, and the British commanders were soon forced to rethink their attitudes about the impenetrability of jungle terrain.

After a tense week of holding, skirmishing and then falling back to new positions about two miles at a time, a regiment of Gurkhas came up and joined the 85th. Bill and his comrades knew these boys were the experts, but looking back, Bill says that it was really too late for them to have done any good by that time.

On guard at a crossroads one night, Bill had a nocturnal encounter that starkly illustrated the expertise of those properly trained in the art of jungle warfare. As Bill stood his watch over the lorries that contained his sleeping comrades in the back of them, a desire to relieve himself came upon him. Bill was quite secure in his belief that they were the only ones present at this crossroads. Given that it seemed quiet enough at the time, Bill thought that he would just quickly nip behind a tree by the road-side. He could still see the lorries from there.

As Bill positioned himself behind the tree and was about to start to answer this call of nature, a hand suddenly grabbed his ankle. 'No, Johnny!' whispered a strange voice.

Bill got the fright of his life! He thought it was a Japanese soldier and hastily pointed his rifle downward, which couldn't have been easy with one hand and the wrong hand at that! In one silent, deft action, Bill's rifle was swept aside and a Gurkha suddenly stood bolt upright in front of him. Bill hadn't seen him at all. In fact, Bill had nearly peed on him, which is why the Gurkha had grabbed his ankle. As soon as recognition had set in, the Gurkha put his finger to his lips in the gesture for silence, handed Bill's rifle back to him and melted back into the darkness of the jungle.

It was fortunate indeed for Bill and his somnolent comrades that the Gurkha wasn't a Japanese soldier instead. Bill had no idea at all that his unit wasn't alone by that crossroads. To this day, Bill doesn't know how many of them were out there, but there certainly had to be more than one and he never saw or heard any of them, despite being on guard. It had also occurred to Bill that the Gurkha had obviously observed Bill's every move, while he remained totally undetected. It was a salutary lesson for the unwary sentry indeed.

The next day saw the men of the 85th in action again. It was during this time that the stark realization that the British didn't actually know how to fight a jungle war really hit home. The Japanese used what Bill and his friends referred to as 'cracker-shells' as a precursor to attack. These shells made a sudden bang, followed by what sounded like several rounds of rifle fire in quick succession. The aim was to confuse the defending troops as to the number and position of the Japanese, and it worked. By the time the British fully understood these disquieting tactics of the Japanese Army it was too late.

Bill recalled that the Japanese used to fire off several of these shells at them while using small gunboats to land parties of about forty or fifty troops in the mangrove swamps behind them. The Japanese seemed to know almost exactly where the British Empire troops were.

Japanese military intelligence was first-rate, but one reason for their success was the fact that they had established an excellent fifth-column all down the Malayan peninsula. Every time the Empire troops set up new gun positions, their presence was betrayed to the Japanese, who simply landed more troops behind them. The Japanese landing parties all had local guides with them as quite a lot of the local people believed the leaflets that the Japanese dropped, telling them that the Japanese soldiers were coming to save them from British rule and exploita-tion. They found out they were wrong later on, of course.

Every one of the British soldiers had been led to believe that the swamps and the jungle were impenetrable. It took the Japanese to prove that line of thinking wrong. The Empire troops soon realized that if they didn't pull back pretty smartly when they heard those cracker-shells, they would be caught in the rapid Japanese pincer movements.

It was during just such a situation that Bill nearly lost two of his friends: Squad Thompson and Jackie Boyce. They'd pulled back so rapidly that afternoon that two of the Battery's valuable 2-pounder guns and their six-man crews simply got left behind! This wasn't realized until the men were missed after the Battery had regrouped. Squad Thompson and Jackie Boyce were together in one of the missing gun crews.

Lieutenant Carpenter was discussing this situation with another officer when Bill interrupted them. 'With your permission sir, I'd like to volunteer to go and get them,' said Bill. Bill knew exactly where to find them as he and Lieutenant Carpenter had reconnoitred the positions for those guns the day before. It was agreed that Bill should take one of the regiment's solo motorcycles and attempt to lead the two gun crews with their lorries back to safety.

As soon as it got dark, Bill took a 500cc BSA and rode off into the jungle. There was no proper road, just a wide track, and he was riding with the headlight masked. He didn't know if the Japanese had already advanced and seized the gun positions or if they were in the jungle around him. He just rode there as fast as he could and hoped that he'd be in time to save his mates.

As it transpired, Bill's arrival was indeed timely. He quickly explained the situation to the two gun crews and the highly mobile 2-pounder guns were quickly made ready for transport. Bill then led his little convoy back along the jungle track he'd used to get to them. As Bill had not encountered anybody on his way to the guns, he thought they would have an uneventful trip back. He really thought that they'd got away with it, but you can imagine his surprise when they suddenly came under fire. Shots rang out in the darkness all around them. Bill quickly extinguished the masked lamps on his motorcycle and took a brief glance over his shoulder. He could see that the two lorries had turned their lights off too, so he just opened the throttle, put his head down and hoped for the best!

With an increasing amount of rifle fire being directed at him plus the two lorries bearing down on him, Bill's situation was not exactly enviable. Suddenly, Bill noticed the muzzle-flash from a rifle almost directly in front of him. Bill remembers thinking: 'He'll be working the bolt for the next one, and that bullet might not miss.' He reacted instantly, aiming the bike almost straight at his would-be killer with the throttle open wide. Bill thinks that the attacker must have thought better of it and moved out of the way. With the two lorries tearing after the motorcycle too, there wouldn't have been much of a chance for the gunman to escape being run over if he'd stayed where he was.

Despite the odds, Bill's little convoy, perhaps more by luck than judgement, got through remarkably unscathed, with one or two extra vent-holes in the lorries, but no casualties. Upon safely rejoining their regiment, Bill reported to Lieutenant Carpenter.

Bill duly received a field promotion to the rank of King's Bombardier, (the Royal Artillery's equivalent of a corporal) for the above exploit. Bill said that it was a great feeling to 'put up a stripe', especially as the field promotion, and of course the increase in pay, were effective immediately.

It was only somewhat later that Bill got a suspicion that it possibly wasn't Japanese troops that had opened fire on them after all. It was highly likely that they had in fact come under fire from some of their own troops! It seems that some retreating British Empire troops had reported firing on a small column of 'Japanese vehicles' at about the same time and in roughly the same area. If such was the case, those retreating Empire soldiers had obviously been unpleasantly surprised by Bill's little convoy coming at them through the jungle and, in the darkness and confusion, assumed them to be Japanese, as they were of course coming from the same direction that any advancing Japanese troops would have been. It was a good job for those in Bill's little convoy that those troops were such rotten shots, whoever they were!

By about 5 February, the gradual falling back of the British and Empire forces had turned into a full-blown retreat to Singapore. Chaos and confusion reigned supreme and the last thirty-five miles back to Singapore were nothing short of a mad dash. The regiments were all scattered and Bill's unit encountered scores of soldiers who had lost their own regiments. As they travelled along the packed roads, they'd often get these lost soldiers asking them if they'd seen the Argylls or the

Cambridgeshires, or any one of a dozen other regiments from whom they'd become separated. In scenes wholly reminiscent of the BEF's withdrawal from Dunkirk, the roadside was littered with broken and abandoned vehicles and equipment, and the beleaguered troops were constantly harassed from the air by Japanese fighter aircraft.

The retreating soldiers also came upon the bodies of some British and Empire troops who'd been caught up in those rapid pincer movements of the Japanese. The first one they encountered was tied to a tree and had been extensively used by the Japanese for bayonet practice. This grim discovery however, did nothing to prepare the retreating troops for what they encountered a few miles further on. They came across about four or five British soldiers who had all been tied to trees facing the road. What differed with these soldiers was the fact that they'd all had their bellies slashed open and been disembowelled in the standing position, then just left there like that to die. It was quite obvious from the faces of the dead men that they'd suffered indescribable agonies before the end came.

The retreating soldiers slowly began to realize the extremely cruel nature of the enemy they were facing. The morale of the retreating troops might have been low at that point but those awful scenes further hardened the men against the Japanese. Each man now began to think along the same lines; that if the end came, each would take as many Japanese with him as he could.

Chapter Three

FIGHTING RETREAT, INEVITABLE DEFEAT

As soon as they made it back across the causeway to Singapore Island, the causeway itself was blown up. It was partially destroyed to slow the Japanese, but not so badly damaged that it couldn't quickly be repaired if reinforcements magically arrived. As for the 85 Anti-Tank, they were sent up to the RAF base at Seletar, to guard it. Seletar airfield was at the top of a hill overlooking a main road as well as one or two other important byways. It thus afforded a commanding view over the surrounding countryside and made for a good defensive position.

By the time Bill's regiment was sent to guard the place however, there wasn't much left, due to heavy bombing raids by the Japanese. The RAF had all but evacuated the base and gone to Java. A large consignment of Hawker Hurricane fighters had been belatedly shipped to Singapore to bolster the RAF's meagre fighter force. Unfortunately, the Hurricanes had all been destroyed during an air raid on the dockside by Japanese bombers. They hadn't even been un-crated. All that remained of the RAF's fighter force when Bill's regiment got to Seletar was three of the hopelessly outclassed Brewster Buffalos and their determined pilots. Their valiant efforts though were all in vain, as all three were shot out of the skies by Japanese Zero fighters the day after the 85 Anti Tank Regiment arrived.

One thing that Bill's regiment did discover upon their arrival at Seletar was the fact that by some miracle and despite the damage, the station's water supply was still on. After two weeks in the jungle, the chance of taking a shower was too good an opportunity to pass up. Putting it mildly Bill says, they stank! As Bill and his comrades piled into the ablution block and felt the wonderful sting of the hot water on their naked bodies, the Japanese decided to pay them a call.

They hadn't been in the shower more than ten minutes when the Japanese bombed the place again. As the Japanese aircraft roared low across the station bombing and strafing, Bill and about thirty other naked soldiers made the forty-yard dash to the relative safety of the nearest slit trench. Anybody who was injured was probably hurt in the crush as they all dived into the trench on top of one another. The raid was proof once again of the excellent information the Japanese had. The air strike took place within one hour of the regiment's arrival.

The next day, what little remained of the Fleet Air Arm's aircraft and flying personnel were also evacuated from Seletar. Lieutenant Carpenter ordered Bill and his section to clear out the Fleet Air Arm's stores and destroy anything that might be of use to the enemy. Unbeknown to Carpenter, others had already had the same idea.

There wasn't that much left behind, but Bill did find six 4-gallon drums containing sugar. As they were removing them, a working party of Australian troops came back to the stores' building. They'd already cleared most of the stuff out and wanted to know what Bill's men were up to. Bill explained that they too had been ordered to clear the stores. The next thing of course was for Bill to ascertain what the Aussies already had. A trade off then ensued. Bill traded four drums of sugar for five kegs of Navy Rum that the Aussies had 'rescued'. He then took one 4-gallon keg to each of the four gun crews in his section and delivered the fifth one to the officers' billet.

Later that evening, Bill was with his section. They were drinking some of the dark Navy Rum out of their enamel tea mugs when Lieutenant Carpenter came along on a motorcycle. Carpenter stopped the bike and said to Bill: 'Ah, having a brew? Excellent idea!' and got off his motorcycle. 'Help yourself, sir,' said Bill with a grin.

It didn't take Carpenter long to work out that it wasn't tea! Carpenter angrily demanded to know where the rum had come from. Bill explained that it had come from the Fleet Air Arm stores that Carpenter had ordered them to clear, adding that it perhaps might have been useful to the enemy! Bill also explained to Carpenter how he had distributed this unexpected prize and that there was a keg of it for the officers too.

Carpenter could see that the men were not in the least bit drunk, so with a caution to Bill that Navy issue rum is full strength and that he was looking to Bill to keep his men sober, Carpenter finished his unexpected tot and got back on his motorcycle. Aiming a wry smile at Bill, he said, 'Mind you, it is damned decent stuff!' With that, Carpenter kicked the bike's engine into life and went on his way.

It was during their short stay at Seletar that the regiment received word of General Wavell's '. . . we shall fight to the last man and bullet' speech. Bill thought that these were fine words indeed, though unfortunately tempered by the knowledge that General Wavell and the other select members of the top brass who had been 'suffering' in the comfort of the Raffles Hotel for the past two weeks, had all hurriedly caught a plane to India and left General Percival to carry the can for the mess that was bound to follow!

The Japanese had, by this time, begun landing troops in the mangrove swamps on the north-western side of Singapore Island. The huge 15-inch guns that defended Singapore mainly faced south and east, over the sea. The guns could be traversed through 240 degrees and, in fact, they were so and managed to fire over 2,000 shells inland at the advancing Japanese. Unfortunately, those shells were nearly all of the armour-piercing type, for use against battleships. Against infantry, as one Japanese commander is later reputed to have said, 'They made a very great noise and a very big hole, but did very little damage.'

This situation was the epitome of the British-held belief that Singapore could only be carried by a sea-borne invasion, the jungle to the north and the swamps to the west having been deemed impenetrable, of course. Now, as the folly of such a strategy made itself wholly apparent, those at Seletar were forced to begin their withdrawal to Singapore City before the hill, over which Seletar stood sentinel, was encircled by the advancing Japanese.

Bill's regiment set up new positions in the residential district of Mount Pleasant. During peacetime, it was easy to see how the district had got its name, as the large colonial style houses, set in the beautifully lush, green, tree-filled tropical landscape of Singapore, were most charming. Now, in wartime, with the Japanese Army advancing through the streets, it was anything but pleasant for those trying to defend it.

As news of the rapid Japanese advance spread, the civilian occupants of those houses hurriedly fled. They were in such a rush to leave that there were still meals on the tables in some of the houses that the retreating Empire troops now used as defensive positions.

It was in one such defensive position that Bill nearly lost his head, literally. He was on guard at the front of the house with his comrade, Dickey Francis. They had positioned themselves in the monsoon drain, beside the road. Dickey had a tommy gun whilst Bill had a Lewis gun. The Lewis machine gun was a relic of the First World War, but it was handy inasmuch as it took the same bullets as the soldiers' rifles, held in a circular drum on top of the gun. Each drum held 200 rounds. Also, it was better than nothing, as Bill's battery had lost their Bren gun when a mortar bomb hit the carrier earlier. They'd taken the damaged tripod-mount off the wrecked Bren-gun carrier and one of their men had modified it to take the Lewis gun. To make it more stable, he'd shortened the length of the tripod legs by about two-thirds, and coincidentally, this measurement subsequently proved to be a near perfect fit for use in a monsoon drain!

The monsoon drains were bowl-sectioned concrete trenches about four feet wide at the top, three and a half feet deep and they also had a gully in the bottom which was a further eighteen or so inches deep. In February, these drains were perfectly dry and therefore made very good 'trench positions'.

It was while Bill and Dickey Francis were in just such a trench that a Japanese sniper fired on them. The first shot ricocheted off the concrete sill at the top of the drain. Dickey and Bill started to work their way along the trench. The sniper's next shot sent Bill into the bottom of the drain, pouring blood. Luckily for him, the sniper's bullet had merely nicked his right ear lobe and severed the chinstrap of his 'battle-bowler', his Army issue steel helmet. Bill quickly realized that by a miracle, he was not seriously hurt but as he held his hand to his ear, he suddenly began to see red, and it wasn't just the blood!

Staying low, Dickey Francis recovered Bill's steel helmet and put it on the end of the tommy gun's barrel. He gradually raised it level with the top of the drain and moved it away from him, looking for the sniper's muzzle-flash. As two more shots rang out, Francis saw what he was looking for and lowered the helmet.

Turning to Bill, Dickey told him that the sniper was located just to their right, across the road, in the middle tree of a group of five palm trees. The middle tree was the tallest of the five and the sniper was in the top of that one. Bill and Dickey then quickly worked out a plan to settle the sniper's hash.

Dickey took Bill's helmet and moved about twenty feet along the trench. Bill got the Lewis gun ready. At Bill's signal, Dickey raised the helmet on the barrel of the tommy gun to draw the sniper's fire. The sniper took the bait as another shot was aimed at the raised helmet. Bill quickly jammed the tripod legs against the sides of the trench and emptied the entire drum into the top of that palm tree, raking it from left to right and back again. In what was almost one continuous burst of fire, Bill literally cut the top of that tree to shreds! Looking back on it, he supposes that it was a bit wasteful of ammunition, but he freely admits that he was just so angry with the sniper!

After a suitable pause, Bill and Dickey emerged from the drain, cautiously crossed the road to the palm tree and looked up. The sniper had slung a safety net underneath him in the top of the tree. His totally bullet-ridden body was now lying in it, dripping blood onto the ground below. Bill and Dickey just left the dead sniper up there in his makeshift hammock as 'bird food'.

They didn't stay in one position for too long, as the Japanese always seemed to know within a couple of hours, where they were. Every time they dug themselves in, they'd either find themselves under mortar or air attack. If it was a mortar attack, the Japanese used a box-barrage, but it wasn't like the one that British troops usually laid down. Where the British barrage was laid to a fixed pattern and was therefore to a degree predictable, the Japanese would change the actual shape of their box every couple of salvoes or so. If one were on the receiving end of such a barrage, there was no alternative but to clear out quickly as one couldn't predict where the next salvo would land and accordingly sidestep it.

For more important targets, the Japanese relied on air support and their own version of the Germans' 'flying artillery' tactics. Having seen the enemy's position, the spotter plane would do one circuit of it then release smoke while flying another circuit. Within seconds, a squadron of Japanese bombers would come along and unload everything they carried, through the smoke ring. It was extremely effective. Any troops still within that ring when the spotter plane completed it, copped a hell of a packet.

The day after the sniper in the palm tree incident, Bill was on watch with a bandaged ear, by an upstairs window in one of the large colonial style houses. Suddenly, he noticed a Japanese spotter plane flying quite slowly, hedge-hopping along the road that his position overlooked. The pilot was obviously deeply engaged in his task. Bill had the Lewis gun set up at the window and as the Japanese plane flew along at about 150 feet or less, it was just too tempting a target. At that range, Bill felt that he just couldn't miss.

Without being ordered to, Bill raked the low-flying aircraft with a long burst of fire from the Lewis gun. The plane's engine caught fire and down it went, trailing smoke, straight into the ground. Bill was immensely satisfied with his work.

The next thing Bill knew was when a greatly angered Lieutenant Carpenter rushed into the room and shouted at him that he was a 'bloody idiot'. Now the Japanese would know *exactly* where they were. Carpenter further decreed that he was of a mind to shoot Bill himself! As if to fulfil Carpenter's prophesy, their position came under a box-barrage from Japanese mortars within fifteen minutes of the spotter plane's crash.

They quickly packed up and withdrew under fire, to a quieter area. The next job was to tend to the wounded. Although one gun crew had been killed, there was mercifully only one man who was wounded seriously enough to warrant a trip to the field hospital, and that was Gunner Williams. Bill felt sufficiently responsible, as his shooting down of the Japanese aircraft had brought the barrage down on them, to volunteer to drive Williams to the Battery's field hospital nearby.

On the way to the hospital, they came upon a couple of other walking wounded, and picked them up. The last man they picked up was a somewhat battered and dazed Gurkha. He didn't seem to be too badly hurt, but he was a bit insensible and it seemed to Bill that he had difficulty in talking.

Once Bill had checked the wounded in at the field hospital, he had to be a witness as a medical orderly went through the personal effects of the men Bill had brought in. They got a shock when they checked those of the dazed Gurkha. In his side-pack were about twenty pairs of human ears! As they stared at them in disbelief, the medical orderly said that he hoped they were at least all Japanese ears. Bill just remembers thinking that it was a good job the Gurkhas were on our side, not theirs.

The next day, the regiment pulled back from the Mount Pleasant district into the outskirts of Singapore City. The Japanese had already encircled the Bukit Tima area and as Bill's regiment withdrew, everyone's attention was drawn to a large pillar of black smoke coming up from Bukit Tima racecourse. It could be seen for miles but nobody at that time knew what it was. They'd heard no bombardment of the racecourse and the smoke was more like what you'd expect to see from a very large fire, rather than from an explosion.

It wasn't until later, when they met up with some men from a retreating Australian regiment who'd been fighting in that area, that Bill and his mates learned what had happened. The Aussie troopers told them that the Japanese had got about 300 or so prisoners roped together in groups of about twenty men and herded them all into the middle of the racecourse. The prisoners were then dowsed in petrol from a tanker and the Japanese just set fire to them all. The Aussies had seen what took place from their position, through binoculars. It must have been truly horrific.

As the troops withdrew ever closer to the city, a small detachment of Japanese soldiers managed to get into a position behind the 85 Anti-Tank Regiment, and tried to cut off their retreat. These Japanese had managed to hole-up in a house and they had a couple of heavy machine guns with them. Bill's lorry was near the head of the column, following that of another gun crew led by Sergeant Salter, when they all came under fire from the hidden Japanese machine gunners. They were nearly pinned down, but Salter quickly ran back and told Bill that his crew would cover them and that Bill was to get the rest of the men out of there.

They were still very much under fire all the time, but as the rest of the column went round them and started to get out, Bill kept looking back and was amazed to see Salter and his crew smartly unload and manhandle their 2-pounder anti-tank gun into a firing position in front of the house. The Japanese gunners in the house were putting a hell of a lot of lead Salter's way and their gun-shield, which was now facing the house, had sparks from the bullet strikes flying off it all the time.

As Bill's crew were now safe from immediate danger, they stopped and watched as Sergeant Salter and his crew put ten 2-pounder shells into the house in very quick succession. Bill recalled that it was an amazing thing to see as with Japanese machine-gun bullets flying all around them, Sergeant Salter and his crew just sat there and defiantly blasted that house, and the Japanese gunners inside it, into oblivion. Salter's crew then equally calmly made their gun ready for transit and caught up with the rest of the column. Sergeant Salter was subsequently awarded the Military Medal for his display of gallantry in this action.

With the Empire troops withdrawing ever deeper, the Japanese began making nightly air raids on Singapore City. It was mainly the civilian population that suffered the casualties though, not that it bothered the Japanese to any degree. That final week was really a week of wasted effort in terms of trying to defend the city. The Japanese had apparently poisoned the water supply, there was mass bombing by Japanese aircraft and among the civilians, disease was beginning to take a hold. With the poisoned water and the drains and sewers being bomb-damaged, public health never stood much of a chance.

On 13 February, the Japanese took the Alexandra Hospital in the suburbs of the city. Bill heard later from troops that were fighting around there that the advancing Japanese had bayo-neted the patients in their beds. Furthermore, the nurses were all dragged out into the street where they were forcibly and most publicly stripped naked. Each was then subjected to a horrifying and equally public rape ordeal by the Japanese troops, after which they were shot dead in the street.

The steadily advancing Japanese were taking no prisoners of any kind. As they got nearer their prize, the atrocities they committed worsened. The last time Bill drove through Raffles Square there were about 200 heads impaled on the spiked rail-ings round the square. Mostly they were civilians' heads with a few British and Empire soldiers' mixed in. It was an absolutely appalling sight. It was as if the Japanese were hell-bent on some kind of wanton spree of revenge or bloodlust.

Bill had noticed something else equally disturbing in the past few days, too. There were a lot of Sikh troops with them in the Indian Brigade. As the end grew nearer, they began to see a lot less of these Sikhs. Bill wasn't the only one to notice this, either. At the time, they presumed that the Sikhs had been killed fighting to the last, because they were thought to be not unlike the Gurkhas. However, India was resisting British rule at that time and there were many Indian soldiers who decided that they would rather not fire upon a fellow enemy of England. Accordingly, the men of Bill's regiment were in for a nasty surprise later on.

As the Japanese Army tightened its grip on Singapore, the men of the 85 Anti-Tank took up new defensive positions in Halifax Road. It was to be their last stand. By this time, the British and Empire forces were virtually surrounded by the Japanese. They spent what turned out to be their last two days mostly avoiding the attentions of Japanese aircraft by staying in the monsoon drains. The military situation, from the point of view of the British and Empire forces, was thought to be utterly hopeless. They were under near enough constant air and mortar attack by then, but there was still this feeling among the troops that somehow it would turn out all right for them, or that maybe reinforcements would arrive any day now.

On St Valentine's Day 1942, Bill and Dickey Francis were among several men sheltering in the monsoon drain from yet another mortar attack, when the trench received a direct hit from a mortar bomb. The bomb landed a short way up the trench but exploded with enough force to blow several of the soldiers further along the drain.

As the smoke and dust cleared, Dickey Francis pointed out to Bill that he'd been hit. Bill looked down at his right arm and was amazed to see that the sleeve of his jacket was soaked in blood. The funny thing was that the sleeve was undamaged and at that moment, he felt no pain at all.

Bill removed his jacket and discovered that he'd been hit in the elbow. There was a hole about the size of a halfpenny in the flesh and it was a good quarter of an inch deep. It was bleeding quite a lot, but it looked clean enough, so he just stuck a field dressing on it from his side-pack. He thought that perhaps a splinter had caused it, but whatever it was had travelled up the sleeve of his army jacket without making a hole in it.

The next morning, 15 February 1942, at a meeting held in the Ford Motor Company's factory in Singapore, Lieutenant General Percival, Commander-in-Chief of the British and Empire forces in Singapore, was reluctantly forced to sign the formal surrender document in front of an increasingly impatient General Yamashita of the Imperial Japanese Army and his staff. Percival had been dragging the negotiations out, trying to buy a little more time and frankly, praying for a miracle. Now, Yamashita's patience was patently at an end. Yamashita threatened the total annihilation of the British forces if Percival didn't sign immediately. Percival, believing that he now had no choice, finally and reluctantly signed. The ceasefire was duly set to commence at 15:00 hours, local time.

The soldiers in Bill's battery were dumbstruck when they got word of this from Lieutenant Carpenter. They just couldn't believe it and neither could Carpenter. It was a bitter pill for them to have to swallow.

The Japanese however, had gambled that the British would surrender due to the plain and simple fact that the Japanese at that moment, had complete command of the air and the sea, and the British and Empire forces had been forced into a large pocket in Singapore City.

For the British top brass, it must have appeared to all intents and purposes to be a repeat of the Dunkirk situation, except that this time there was no 'armada of little ships' to rescue the beleaguered troops, nowhere to escape to and no prospect of the arrival of reinforcements. Militarily all hope appeared to have been lost long ago. But the British commanders were completely unaware of the Japanese Army's actual situation. Yamashita had good reason to be impatient for Percival to sign the surrender document, as we shall see later. In the meantime, his gamble paid off and General Yamashita made the Ford factory, the scene of his victory and the humiliation of the old colonial powers, his permanent headquarters.

As the ceasefire took effect at 15:00, everybody was ordered to move to Cemetery Road. This was a British order, not a Japanese one. Given the many atrocities already committed against prisoners, the British officers felt that their best chance lay in the old adage of 'safety in numbers' and the bigger the number, the safer they might be.

During this strategic withdrawal, the 85's column was once again caught in an air attack. It was 15:30 hours, half an hour after the ceasefire took effect; Bill's regiment were crossing the bridge at Canning Fort Rise when a small force of Japanese bombers attacked them. Bill made it safely across the bridge with his gun crew and their lorry, but one of the lorries behind them was just crossing when the bridge took a direct hit. In that lorry was the gun crew led by Sergeant Cross. The other members of Cross' crew were Sergeant Clayton, Bombardier Gee, Squad Thompson, Jackie Boyce and Frank Steadman.

Cross, Clayton and Gee were all killed instantly. Sergeant

Cross was killed directly by the blast, whilst flying splinters killed Sergeant Clayton and Bombardier Gee. Nobody knew what happened to Thompson, Boyce and Steadman; they were simply 'missing' from the shattered lorry.

When they got to Cemetery Road, Bill discovered that Sergeant Cross' crew were posted as missing. Later, as others came in, Bill ascertained that the two sergeants and the bombardier had definitely been killed, but there was still no news of the three missing men. The uncertainty over the combined fates of his three missing friends saved Bill's life that evening.

They spent the next couple of hours at Cemetery Road smashing up or de-activating their arms and equipment. Bill was worried about his missing friends, but there was a job to do. He destroyed their 2-pounder gun and the lorry by blowing up the lorry's petrol tank. Once it was thoroughly ablaze, they threw the rifles, pistols, tommy guns and the Lewis gun into the back of the lorry. Others simply ran their loaded lorries into the nearest bomb-crater, before setting fire to them. They were not going to give the Japanese anything remotely useful. Nor were they going to give them the satisfaction of disarming them, either.

At about 17:00 hours, Lieutenant Carpenter had two visitors. Captain Greville and Lieutenant Hatchett from the Battery Headquarters staff came to him with a plan to take a lorry and make a break for it. They wanted Carpenter to go with them as a spare driver. They planned to break out along the lightly guarded causeway and try to make it to Burma. They already had a lorry with a full petrol tank and they had several more gallons of fuel in cans in the back of it. What they didn't know was that Burma was already in Japanese hands.

In the event, Carpenter turned them down. His men were scattered and half of Sergeant Cross' gun crew were still missing. Lieutenant Carpenter felt a great responsibility towards his men. He also felt that he owed it to them to remain with them.

On Carpenter's recommendation, Greville and Hatchett approached Bill, to see if he would go. Bill told Hatchett that three of his mates were in that missing gun crew and that he couldn't go without at least knowing about them for certain. Hatchett and Greville told Bill that he had until 19:00 hours to decide. 'At 19:00, we are going, with or without you, Bombardier,' said Greville. The two men then left to finalize their preparations.

At the appointed hour, there was still no news of the three missing men. Hatchett and Greville took their lorry and their chances and left. At 19:30, Thompson, Boyce and Steadman finally trudged wearily into camp and were reunited with a delighted Bill Reed.

The three men had all managed to jump out of the back of the lorry as it was hit, into the river below. By the time they climbed out of the water, they realized that they'd have to walk to Cemetery Road. The Japanese meanwhile, had caught Hatchett and Greville on the causeway. They were both killed in the subsequent exchange of fire.

Shortly after the missing men had turned up, it was decided that everybody ought to try to find a suitable place to bed down for the night. Dusk was approaching as Bill and Squad decided to look in the bombed-out houses across the street for anything that might be useful. In an upstairs bedroom of one of the houses, they discovered a wardrobe full of clothes. By this time, their uniforms were not much more than rotten rags. Bill found a green silk shirt, a pair of green cotton trousers and joy of joys, some clean underwear! He felt very fine, though of course he still had to wear what remained of his bloodstained army jacket over the top of these clothes.

Squad found the sprung bedstead of a double bed in another house. The two men managed to get it down the bomb damaged staircase and took it across the road to the cemetery, where they balanced it on two graves. They spread their groundsheets over it and, with their army blankets on top of them, Bill and Squad were quite cosy.

As the two men lay there on their makeshift bed atop the graves staring up into the star-speckled sky, Squad said to Bill that if they 'copped it' that night, they were at least in the right place!

'The right place?' pondered Bill. Somehow he doubted that. The much vaunted but fatally flawed fortress island of Singapore, bastion of the British Empire, was now securely in Japanese hands. Tomorrow, they would march into captivity.

Chapter Four

PRISONER OF THE JAPANESE

The morning after the capitulation was strangely quiet. There were no bombardments, no air attacks and no mortar barrages but, as the day wore on, they began to hear distant rifle and machine-gun fire. Unbeknown to the men, a contingent of their Japanese captors had started an impromptu programme to exterminate the local Chinese civilian population.

That afternoon, the men were formed up and marched to Roberts Barracks, near Changi, escorted by a few Japanese guards on bicycles. As the column of defeated and dejected men marched through the war-torn streets of Singapore, they noticed that there were dead bodies everywhere. Some were casualties of the earlier Japanese air raids; they could tell they'd been there a little while. But there were an awful lot of very fresh ones. They hadn't all been shot either; some had been beheaded. The captured men began to wonder what was in store for them.

As the captured troops marched along, some of the local people tried to pass food to them in the form of fresh fruit or vegetables, or cheese. But if the Japanese guards saw them do it, they turned on them and beat them up by the roadside.

Upon arrival at Roberts Barracks, the men were largely left to their own devices. It appeared to Bill that the Japanese didn't know quite what to do with all the prisoners. There were so many of them; thousands in fact. At first, the British officers organized working parties to establish a hospital area for the many wounded among their number who had been brought along on handcarts or rickshaws. They daren't leave the wounded behind, as they knew only too well what was likely to

36

happen to them. Fortunately, there were a lot of RAMC (Royal Army Medical Corps) personnel in the large group of captured soldiers now massed at Roberts Barracks.

As well as trying to construct a usable hospital, the men also had to build some sort of accommodation for themselves at the bombed-out barracks. Squad found a hut that would do for a group of them. They then went foraging for some materials to make it liveable. Bill went into what used to be the base cinema and started tearing out the seats. He then broke the curved backs off the chairs and these were used as beds: crude, but it worked.

Wednesday, 18 February 1942 was in fact Bill's twenty-first birthday. Lying on his cinema-seat bed that evening after the day's work and looking up at the stars where the roof should have been, he suddenly remarked upon that fact. 'Some twenty-first birthday this is!' he said to nobody in particular. On hearing this despairing throwaway remark of Bill's, Squad quickly got up and left the makeshift hut.

He returned a few minutes later with about thirteen others and they held an impromptu party. The food consisted of hard-tack biscuits, a tin of pilchards and a tin of pineapple rings. For drink, they had chocolate made from somebody's K-rations and the syrup from the tin of pineapple. That was Bill's coming of age! He now officially had the 'key to the door', only there was no door. The Japanese had blown it to pieces!

They spent a further week building the hospital and their own accommodation. During this time, they saw remarkably few Japanese guards. The men were pretty much free to come and go on their foraging expeditions, but on the Wednesday after Bill's birthday, barriers were set up on the roads around Roberts Barracks. There was a lot of very audible murmuring going on among the prisoners, when somebody came into Bill's hut and asked him if he'd seen the new guards that had arrived and were now manning those barriers. Bill said he hadn't, so they all went outside to see what the fuss was about. You can imagine their shocked surprise when they saw that their guards were not Japanese soldiers. They were the missing Sikh troops from their own Brigade. The Sikhs had changed sides.

The atmosphere was quite menacing for a while. The turncoat

Sikh guards were doing their best to ignore the derisive calls and the scowls that were directed at them from their former comrades in arms. Bill recalled that as the turncoats were now guarding them and were all armed, of course, they couldn't do much about it. But the Gurkhas, when they saw them, would go right up to their faces to leer at them, and then slowly draw a finger across their own throat, in a gesture that said it all.

Two weeks after capture, the living conditions for the prisoners at Roberts Barracks still could not even be described as basic. The prisoners had done their best to make the bombed-out barracks habitable, but there was still no fresh water supply and the latrines were merely open cesspits. The army rations that the prisoners had brought with them had run out within the first few days.

The prisoners had to send a party daily to collect their food allowance from nearby Selarang Barracks. To feed their captives, the Japanese provided a daily food allowance consisting of the carcass of half a water buffalo, five or six sacks of low-grade rice and two or three sacks of sweet potatoes. With this, the men had to make a stew for the 2,000 plus prisoners held in Roberts Barracks.

In order to cook the stew, the prisoners used the large 'coppers' in the former barracks' laundry, but before they could boil the rice, they had to first sterilize the water. As there was no fresh water supply, they had to fetch a lot of seawater from Changi beach and boil the salt out of it. They would save the salt residue too. The prisoners also had to use boiled seawater to make something resembling tea. The first mug of this so-called tea would have to be drunk quickly, to avoid its rather saline flavour. The next mug was the daily allowance for washing and shaving. Bill recalls that the prisoners used to celebrate whenever it rained as it meant that they had fresh water. The men used to catch it in groundsheets, mugs, buckets; anything they could find. It really was a priceless commodity.

Not surprisingly, the prisoners foraged for food, with which to supplement their meagre rations, outside of the camp. It was on one such expedition that Bill and some of the others witnessed at first hand, soldiers of the Japanese Army at work.

Bill was among about half a dozen prisoners who were out foraging one morning. They'd gone down to Changi beach to collect coconuts. Suddenly, they heard the sound of lorries coming. The foragers hid in the denser foliage under the palm trees as three Japanese Army trucks came along the road. They were worried what the Japanese might do to them if they saw prisoners this far from camp. They also thought that the Japanese might take their precious coconuts.

The lorries passed the hidden men, drove onto the beach and stopped. Bill and the other members of the foraging party watched as the Japanese soldiers dropped the tailboards and ordered the people in the back of the three lorries to climb down onto the beach. They each had about twenty-five male Chinese civilian prisoners in the back of them, all manacled. The Japanese soldiers ordered them into the sea, till they were at waist level in the water. Bill wondered exactly what the Japanese soldiers were up to. He didn't have to wait long for the answer.

Horror-struck, Bill and his comrades watched what happened as the Japanese soldiers just machine-gunned the Chinese prisoners in the water. When it was over, the laughing soldiers all got back into their lorries and drove off, leaving the outgoing tide to dispose of the bodies.

For the first month of captivity, the Japanese still left the British prisoners to their own devices. But on the meagre rations allowed them, the prisoners' health deteriorated rapidly. Their newly imposed diet of rice stew had little vitamin or protein content and as well as weight loss, other conditions began to appear. Dysentery was the first to make itself known, followed inevitably by malaria. The weakened men quickly proved susceptible to both and many of them died of these treatable diseases purely for lack of proper food and medication.

About six weeks after he'd been captured, Bill developed an eye condition. The lack of vitamins in his diet had caused corneal ulcers to form. Bill went virtually blind and was now admitted to the hospital that he had helped to build. He wasn't the only one by any means. There were more than forty of them with this complaint in the hospital. All were put in the care of Colonel Rose, an Australian eye specialist.

With no proper medicines available, Colonel Rose's team had to resort to some extremely basic techniques in their efforts to cure their patients. The treatment consisted of an orderly putting drops of cocaine into the eyes, to deaden them a little, ready for the next bit. Then they'd swab the eyes out with some kind of oily cleanser that was applied liberally with a paintbrush. The patients never did find out what the cleanser was, but it slowly started to work and they begin to see light and shade, though always through a misty, murky film.

Colonel Rose had the floor areas around his patients' beds painted white. As the men slowly regained some semblance of their sight, he would get each of them up in turn and stand the patient at the foot of his bed. He would then stand about fifteen feet in front of the patient and tell him to walk slowly toward him, saying: 'Tell me when you see something.' As soon as the patient gave the indication, Rose would stop him and draw a line at his feet. The patient's progress was thus measured by the series of lines on the floor.

While Bill was in the hospital, the fitter men in Roberts Barracks were moved out to Singapore's River Valley camp. The hungry prisoners were put to work emptying food warehouses and loading the merchandise onto Japanese Army lorries. The prisoners stole what little food they could, but the penalties if they were caught were severe. The very least a prisoner could expect to get away with was a savage beating from the Japanese guards.

By about the end of June 1942, word filtered through to those in the hospital at Roberts Barracks that the men at River Valley had been sent up country to northern Malaya, to build new prison camps with much better food and conditions. The men in the hospital were greatly heartened by this news. Squad Thompson, Jackie Boyce and Frank Steadman were among the first batch of men from River Valley to be sent.

Bill was discharged from the hospital in September. He was given a pair of dark anti-flash goggles of the type used by Bren gunners, to protect his eyes. They were a great help to him and Bill kept them with him for a long time afterwards. In fact, they were almost his most treasured possession and he must have repaired them dozens of times before they finally had to be thrown away. Newly discharged, Bill was put onto light duties such as fetching seawater or collecting bamboo. Gradually, the Japanese managed to restore the water supply to Roberts Barracks.

It was about this time that Colonel Lardener-Clarke was made to sign a 'no escapes promise' on behalf of all the men at Roberts Barracks. He signed it very much under duress. The Sikh guards left and were replaced by Japanese soldiers. The regime change at Roberts Barracks brought the kind of harshness that the prisoners would come to know only too well in the coming months and years.

The first incidence of this regime materialized when one day, in a blaze of defiance, the Gurkhas in the camp refused to work for the Japanese. Trouble wasn't long in coming. About twenty Japanese soldiers went into the Gurkhas' quarters and dragged two randomly selected men out of each hut. Then they systematically broke each victim's arms and legs with their rifle butts. The poor victims were then picked up by their now broken limbs and bodily thrown back into their hut. This went on every morning with fresh victims until the Gurkhas changed their minds, which took about a week. Then they joined the work details.

One morning in October, the men were assembled and a Japanese officer told them: 'All men go north to new camp. Better food. Better conditions. Nippon army take care of prisoners.' The prisoners were then taken by lorry to Singapore railway station. They began to think that what they had heard before was obviously true. Even when they were herded like cattle into the covered metal wagons of the train, the men didn't mind so much because they thought that they'd soon be there and then it would all be all right.

The train left Singapore station and began an arduous journey north that would last for four days and five nights. There would be only one main stop per day, when the prisoners would be allowed to get out of the overcrowded wagons. The journey was tortuously slow and the train made frequent stops in sidings to

41

allow other trains to pass on the single-track line. The heat inside those metal wagons during the day was unbearable. At night, the temperature dropped to what felt like freezing point.

God help anyone that had dysentery, as a lot of them did. If it struck, and you were lucky, your mates would hold on to you as you stuck your backside out of the open door while the train was in motion. If not, you had no option but to sit in it. After four days and five nights, the stench in those wagons was over-powering and many men didn't survive the journey.

The train finally reached its destination; a place called Ban Pong, on the edge of the jungle region of Thailand (known as Siam until 1939). This was the base camp and it consisted of about thirty acres of black, waterlogged, stinking mud with long, crudely-built dormitory-style huts in the middle of it. The camp's latrines consisted of large open trenches with bamboo poles slung across upon which users sat. Due to the rains, these trenches were already overflowing into the camp, which was the reason for the colour and aroma of the mud. The huts were simply bamboo shelters with a roof of thatched palm (attap) and they had no sides to them. The floors of these huts were sort of raised platforms of duck boards, laid in a vain attempt to stop the encroachment of the stinking black morass from the over-flowing latrine trenches. The whole place was a bacteriologist's dream come true.

On seeing their new surroundings, most of the men thought: 'This can't be right, can it?' A few even braved the wrath of their Japanese guards and asked where the new camp with better food and conditions was. The reply, delivered with a demonic grin from the few guards who spoke any kind of English was: 'This camp! Now all men work hard, every day! All men work hard for the Emperor!'

Amid the laughter of the guards, the prisoners waded through the foul quagmire to their new accommodation. Their first task was to attempt to bury those of their comrades who had not survived the train journey from Singapore. There would be thousands more prisoners who would not survive the living hell that was to follow.

Chapter Five

THE RAILWAY OF DEATH

Their rapid conquest of south-east Asia had left the Japanese with a big problem; the re-supply of their conquering forces. At that time, the only route between Singapore and Rangoon, in Burma, was a 2,000-mile sea voyage around the Malay Peninsula. That in itself meant delays, but the added menace from American submarines and long-range bombers meant that Japanese ships faced a hazardous passage to say the least. Indeed, quite a number of their ships were lost on the protracted voyage, so valuable supplies were not reaching the Japanese troops. The Japanese badly needed an alternative route.

In 1929, the British had surveyed a route for a railway linking Bangkok and Rangoon. The only route remotely possible was a 250-mile line through the most inhospitable terrain imaginable. The proposed line would have to run through miles of dense, virgin jungle, across plains on long embankments and rivers and streams on bridges that would have to cope with sudden and dramatic flooding during the monsoon season. It would have to run round mountains, as well as through deep cuttings that would have to be made through solid rock in some places. It was a mammoth civil engineering project that would take an estimated three years to complete. The original plan was to start from both ends of the line simultaneously and meet somewhere in the middle. But the project also came with a hefty price tag and the original surveyor's report concluded that the proposed railway was not a viable proposition, so the project was duly abandoned.

In the late spring of 1942, the Japanese Army resurrected the scheme. They certainly appreciated the difficulties but they had the skilled engineers needed to undertake such a project and, although they did not possess the necessary heavy plant, the Japanese, like the ancient Egyptians before them, had a wealth of slave labour. The Emperor's railway would thus be built in the same manner as the Great Pyramids had been. As the many thousands of Allied prisoners of war were also totally expendable as far as the Japanese were concerned, it would certainly solve the problem of what to do with them all. To the Japanese, not only was the building of the 250-mile Burma-Thailand railway now suddenly feasible, it was also very necessary.

The existing state railways of Burma and Thailand already had suitable railheads. All that was necessary, as far as the Japanese were concerned, was to link them through the jungle, following the line of a particular river, the Kwai Noi. At the Burma end, the railhead was at Moulmeim, which had a direct line to Rangoon. In Thailand, a junction would be made at Ban Pong, just west of Non Pladuk, with the existing line to Bangkok. The Japanese were looking forward to building this railway for their Emperor and in a lot less time than the British had originally envisaged, as the Japanese planned to start the line's construction simultaneously in about sixteen to twenty places along the proposed route, each camp working in both directions toward each other.

The prisoners of war didn't have any idea what their captors were up to at that time but Bill had been at Ban Pong for only a short time when the Japanese came in one morning and started calling some of them out by name. Somehow or other, they'd obtained the men's army records and they were seeking out anyone who had knowledge relevant to construction work. Bill's army record showed that he was an apprentice stonemason and builder, with army knowledge and training in the use of explosives.

About twenty of the prisoners were hand picked that morning, put into a lorry and taken up to Kanchanaburi. There they were transferred to a supply barge that headed off up river; a far easier passage than that of the men who had been the very first to be sent. They had been force-marched through the dense jungle for

1. Men of 251 Battery at Clacton prior to embarkation aboard SS *Narkunda*.
   Front row seated: 7th from left is BSM Ben Pritchett, 9th from left is Lieutenant Carpenter. Seated behind his dog is Major Turrell, Battery Major.
   2nd row down from top: 4th from left is Squad Thompson, 5th from left, next to Thompson is Bill Reed. *(Photo: Bill Reed.)*

2. Gunner Bill Reed, just before the outbreak of war. *(Photo: Bill Reed.)*

3. Ben Pritchett at
   the time of the
   motorcycle race at
   Benham Park
   camp.
   (Photo: Ben Pritchett.)

4. Ben as Battery
   Sergeant Major, in
   Singapore.
   (Photo: Ben Pritchett.)

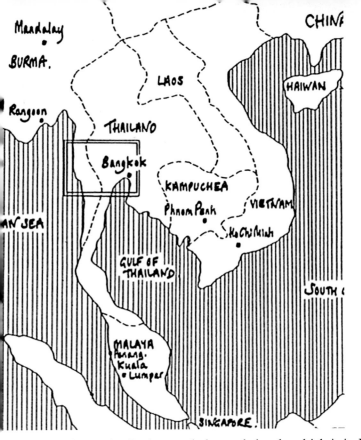

5. Map of Burma, Thailand and Malaya showing area of the Burma-Thailand Railway. *(Courtesy of Jack Cosford.)*

6. Detail from a badly damaged charcoal sketch, which is in Bill's possession. The sketch was based on Sugano at Tarsao camp and was drawn by a fellow prisoner. *(Photo: Bill Reed.)*

7. War graves cemetery at Chungkai, Thailand. *(Photo: via Bill Reed.)*

8. Engine No. C 5623, formerly used by the Japanese on the Burma-Thailand Railway, now preserved at Kanchanaburi visitor centre. *(Photo: via Bill Reed.)*

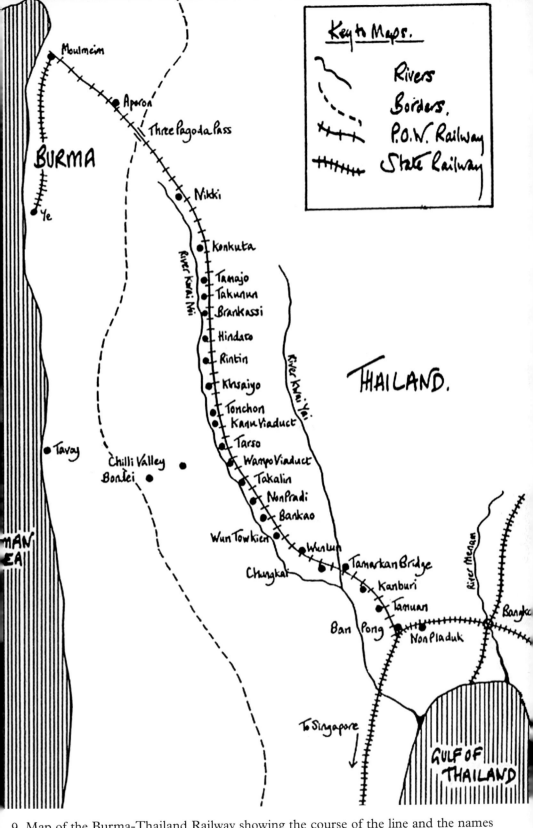

9. Map of the Burma-Thailand Railway showing the course of the line and the names and locations of all the prison camps. *(Courtesy of Jack Cosford.)*

10. Tamarkan Bridge as it is today.

(Photo: *via Bill Reed.*)

11. Modern day diesel train crossing Tamarkan Bridge. *(Photo: via Bill Reed.)*

12. Site where Tonchan camp once stood.   *(Photo: via Bill Reed.)*

13. The remains of Wampo viaduct. The viaduct originally carried the line at a height of about 200 feet, which is the ridgeline of the rock above the viaduct in this picture. Trains still use the viaduct today, although there is a 10mph speed restriction.

(Photo: via Bill Reed.)

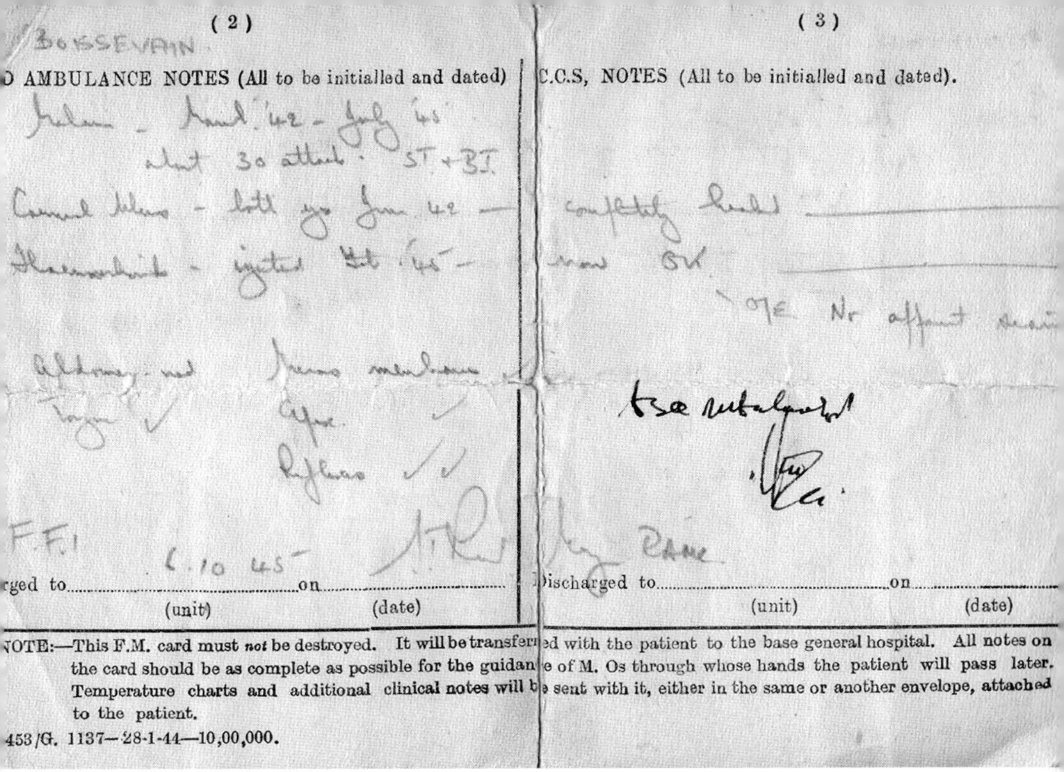

(2)

BOISSEVAIN

D AMBULANCE NOTES (All to be initialled and dated)

F.F.I

1.10.45

rged to..................................on..................................

(unit) (date)

(3)

C.C.S, NOTES (All to be initialled and dated).

Discharged to..................................on..................................

(unit) (date)

NOTE:—This F.M. card must *not* be destroyed. It will be transferred with the patient to the base general hospital. All notes on the card should be as complete as possible for the guidance of M. Os through whose hands the patient will pass later. Temperature charts and additional clinical notes will be sent with it, either in the same or another envelope, attached to the patient.

453/G. 1137—28-1-44—10,00,000.

14 – 15. Field medical card issued to Bill aboard the MV *Boissevain* on his way home.
(Photo: Bill Reed.)

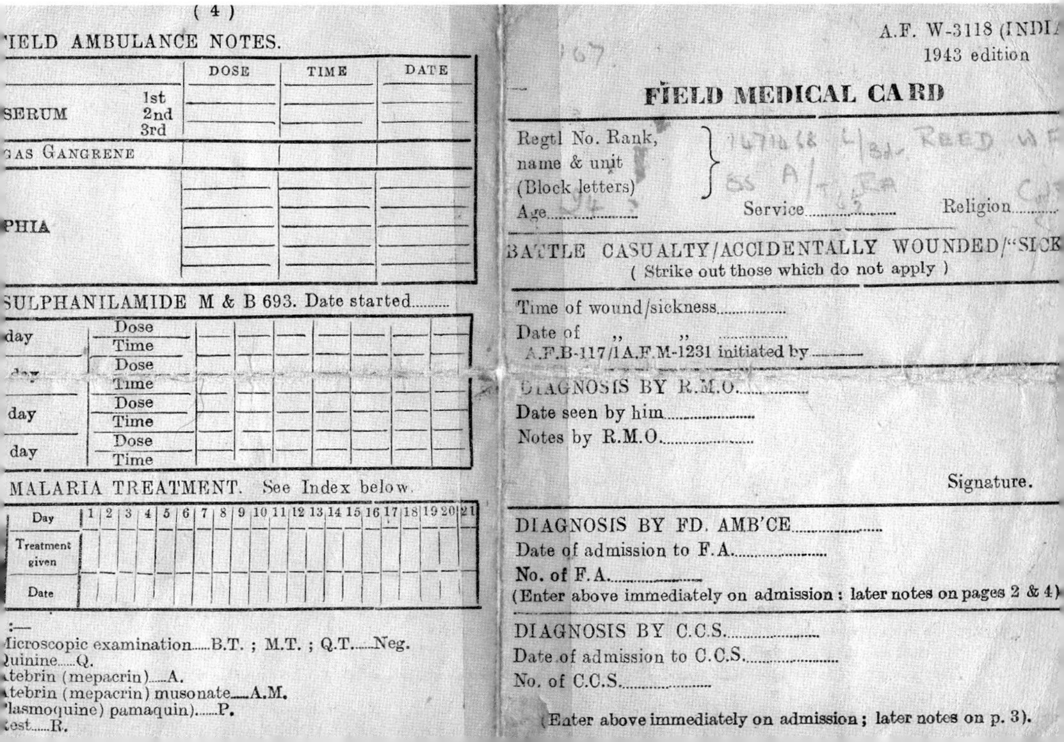

(4)

FIELD AMBULANCE NOTES.

		DOSE	TIME	DATE
SERUM	1st			
	2nd			
	3rd			
GAS GANGRENE				
PHIA				

SULPHANILAMIDE M & B 693. Date started..........

day	Dose								
	Time								
day	Dose								
	Time								
day	Dose								
	Time								
day	Dose								
	Time								

MALARIA TREATMENT. See Index below.

Day	1	2	3	4	5	6	7	8	9	10	11	12	13	14	15	16	17	18	19	20	21
Treatment given																					
Date																					

:—
Microscopic examination.....B.T. ; M.T. ; Q.T.....Neg.
Quinine.....Q.
Atebrin (mepacrin).....A.
Atebrin (mepacrin) musonate.....A.M.
Plasmoquine) pamaquin).....P.
Rest.....R.

A.F. W-3118 (INDIA
1943 edition

FIELD MEDICAL CARD

Regtl No. Rank, name & unit (Block letters) } 14714 L/Bdr. REED W.F. 85 A/T RA
Age..24.. Service..........5.. Religion..........C of E

BATTLE CASUALTY/ACCIDENTALLY WOUNDED/"SICK
(Strike out those which do not apply)

Time of wound/sickness..........
Date of " " ....
A.F.B-117/IA.F.M-1231 initiated by..........

DIAGNOSIS BY R.M.O..........
Date seen by him..........
Notes by R.M.O..........

Signature.

DIAGNOSIS BY FD. AMB'CE..........
Date of admission to F.A..........
No. of F.A..........
(Enter above immediately on admission; later notes on pages 2 & 4)

DIAGNOSIS BY C.C.S..........
Date of admission to C.C.S..........
No. of C.C.S..........

(Enter above immediately on admission; later notes on p. 3).

16. The Harris family. *Top:* Beryl's parents, Alf and Rosanna. *Bottom right:* Beryl Harris; *bottom left:* her sister, Ivy. *(Photos: Beryl Reed.)*

17. Bill and Beryl on their wedding day. Squad Thompson was best man.

(Photo: Bill Reed.)

18. Bill Reed working as a stonemason at Knole House, a National Trust property in Sevenoaks, Kent. *(Photo: via Bill Reed.)*

19. Bill and Beryl on their Ruby Wedding anniversary with their beloved German Shepherd dog, Sheba. *(Photo: Bill Reed.)*

20. Bill and Beryl with their sons, daughters-in-law and grandchildren. *(Photo: Bill Reed.)*

21. A recent photo of Bill with Badger and Goldie in his garden at Allhallows.
(Photo: Bill Reed.)

22. Bill receiving the RSPCA medal from Lady Victoria De Trafford, for his rescue of a sheepdog from a well. Bill's mother is standing to his left. It was this medal that Bill traded in captivity by passing it off as an Olympic Gold Medal. *(Photo: via Bill Reed.)*

23. Bill with the replacement medal that the RSPCA gave to him years later. *(Photo: via Bill Reed.)*

24. *Left to right:* Cyril Hullcup, Ben Pritchett and Dickey Francis, pictured at Bill and Beryl's Golden Wedding Anniversary.

IN HONOURED REMEMBRANCE OF THE FORTITUDE AND
SACRIFICE OF THAT VALIANT COMPANY WHO PERISHED
WHILE BUILDING THE RAILWAY FROM THAILAND TO BURMA
DURING THEIR LONG CAPTIVITY

THOSE WHO HAVE NO KNOWN GRAVE ARE COMMEMORATED
BY NAME AT RANGOON SINGAPORE AND HONG KONG AND
THEIR COMRADES REST IN THE THREE WAR CEMETERIES
OF KANCHANABURI CHUNGKAI AND THANBYUZAYAT

*I will make you a name and a praise among all people of the earth
when I turn back your captivity before your eyes, saith the LORD*

25 Plaque of remembrance for those prisoners who died building the railway, at the Kanchanaburi war cemetery.

days to each of the proposed locations and many of them had not survived the trek.

The supply barge was loaded with picks, shovels, hammers, taps, about a dozen Japanese engineers and the twenty prisoners. At each of the first four main camps up river, five prisoners and either one or two of the engineers were dropped off. The drops in order were: Chungkai, Wampo and Tarsao. Bill and the four remaining specialists in his group were dropped off last, at Tonchan camp.

In this last group were Sergeant Cyril Hullcup, from Bill's regiment, Sergeant Way, a Malay volunteer who in peacetime was a mining engineer, 'Juddy' Edge and Andy Inglis, who were quarrymen in peacetime and, of course, Bill.

On the small landing stage at Tonchan, parties of prisoners were waiting to unload the supply boat. As he stepped onto the jetty, the first person Bill saw was Jackie Boyce. They daren't 'jump for joy' at their reunion as the guards were watching, but Boyce did manage to tell Bill that Squad Thompson and Frank Steadman were also at Tonchan camp, as were about twenty others from 251 Battery, including the Battery Sergeant Major, Ben Pritchett. Bill was delighted to find his old comrades again. They managed to have a more relaxed reunion later on, without the Japanese breathing down their necks.

Bill and the other four specialists were detailed to work with the Japanese engineers. On the high ground 100 feet above the river, the prisoners had already cleared about 200 square yards of virgin jungle and been made to build their own and their captors' accommodation during the preceding three months.

The five specialists were usually kept together and away from the other prisoners whenever possible. It was quickly noticed that there was something different about their guards. Bill enquired of some of the other prisoners about them and was told that their guards were not Japanese, despite the uniforms. They were Koreans, and rather nasty ones at that. Bill was warned that they'd better watch out.

Initially, Bill and his group of specialists were put on surveying duties. The other prisoners had the backbreaking task of clearing the path of the line through the jungle. Bill's group worked for twelve hours a day, with one day in ten off. It was during this time that they discovered they were building a railway. Bill's group were heading north from Tonchan toward Three Pagodas Pass, which is where the new railway would cross the Burma-Thailand border. There were always four Japanese engineers and four very mean-looking Korean guards with them while they were out working.

Despite the close attentions of the guards, Bill and his mates always managed to shift their marker pegs and thereby confuse the Japanese surveyors' theodolite readings. This was to have a remarkably profound effect later, as the parties working south from the Burma end linked up with the parties working northward in the region of a place called Nikki-Nikki.

When that particular link-up came, the two paths were about 100 yards apart in an east-west direction. It seems that the specialists in the southern working party had been doing exactly the same as those of Bill's group; shifting the surveying pegs. There was an awful lot of what Bill calls 'Jap-Flapping' (shouting and face-slapping) going on between the Japanese officers and the soldiers of each party when this situation became apparent.

But it didn't end there. While the prisoners were all laughing inwardly at the situation and thoroughly enjoying the spectacle of the guards being slapped about by their junior officers, the more senior Japanese officers sent for the dreaded Kempeitai; the Japanese equivalent of the German Gestapo. When the prisoners saw the Kempeitai arrive, the mood changed very quickly. Bill recalled that they really thought they were for it!

But Bill and his comrades were about to witness another strange facet of the Japanese psyche. The Kempeitai left the prisoners completely alone! Instead, they took the engineers away, their own people, and beat them to a pulp. Then they took the chief engineer, who Bill says was actually a nice chap for a Jap, beat him up and shot him. They'd blamed him for the whole thing! Bill can't remember his name. He couldn't pronounce it anyway, but he and the other prisoners always called him 'Itchy Cow-son', as that was the nearest they could be bothered to get to pronouncing it. 'Itchy' always used to give the specialists in his team cigarettes, and Bill and his friends missed those afterwards.

The prisoners' efforts in confusing the surveying work caused only a minor delay in the punishing schedule to meet the railway's completion date, which the Japanese had set as 15 August 1943, but as Bill recalls, it was immensely satisfying for them to watch the Japanese having to backtrack both ends to straighten it all out!

The surveying work ended by Christmas 1942. Bill thinks that the Japanese were almost pleased with the railway's progress at that point. Track had already been laid at Ban Pong and the line had progressed as far north as Chungkai. But that first part of the railway's construction had been comparatively easy as the terrain up to Chungkai was mainly flat, open plains, or paddy fields. After that, things got a lot harder.

On Christmas day 1942, the commandant of Tonchan camp, Sergeant Tora 'Tiger' Hiramatsu, granted the prisoners an extra 'yasumi' day. (Yasumi means 'rest' in Japanese.) They even got an extra food allowance, which actually contained fresh eggs. This was luxury indeed, all apparently courtesy of Tiger Hiramatsu.

Bill states that Tiger was not, as he put it, 'your typical Jap'. He was about four feet, nine inches tall, stocky, ox-like even, with very hard facial features. He was a strict disciplinarian and he could be extremely hard, but he certainly wasn't a sadist, unlike many of the other Japanese. Tiger was, at that time, quite old for a sergeant. Bill thinks he was about forty and he'd been very much a career soldier. He was intensely patriotic, so his duty to his Emperor and his country always came first and he lived very much by a strict code of honour, but he could sometimes be very bad tempered. It wasn't until a little later, when some of the prisoners realized how much pressure he was under from his superiors, that a lot of them actually began to understand this rather enigmatic soldier.

It is worth a slight digression, since the word 'yasumi' has now been introduced, to explain why Japanese words will now increasingly come into the text of this story.

Only a few of the Japanese at the camp actually spoke any kind of English. At first, they'd tried to force the prisoners to speak Japanese, without the benefit of any coaching! The initial result was that the prisoners led quite a few Japanese and Korean guards to believe that their surname, translated into English, was 'bastard'; very entertaining at first as various guards ran around the camp smiling and telling anyone who would listen, 'me Mr Bastard'. It was a statement with which the prisoners unquestionably agreed, but the camp interpreter soon put the guards right, which more often than not resulted in retribution.

By that first Christmas, quite a few of the Japanese and Koreans had picked up a broken form of the English language, including the more popular swear words, and the prisoners in turn had picked up a broken form of Japanese. The result was a strange hybrid language that they all called 'Japlish' and it actually served the purpose most of the time. It is an interesting side-effect of his time as a prisoner that, today, Bill can actually count faster in Japanese than he can in his native English. Of course, in the camps, he had to. They all did unless they wanted a beating.

Among the 2,000 or so prisoners at Tonchan that Christmas, was a man called L.B. John. He had been a professional boxer before the war, but the prejudice of the time meant that because he was not white, he was not permitted to contend for any British title, despite beating the then British middleweight champion, Ronnie James, in an unofficial bout.

On their unexpected bonus yasumi day, John was sparring with somebody for the benefit of the men out in the camp's compound, when Tiger Hiramatsu saw them. Tiger enquired of the prisoners what was going on. Once informed, he stopped the sparring session, as an idea occurred to him. He then told L.B. John, via the camp's interpreter, a Japanese soldier who was actually of mixed blood, that he wanted him to teach the Korean guards how to box.

Without a moment's hesitation, Tiger had one of the Koreans brought to John. 'Now, fight!' said Tiger. Bill recalls that L.B. John looked quite worried by this. At first he hardly hit the guard and Tiger looked more than a bit puzzled by this. Tiger stopped the charade, shouting: 'Nai! (No) Hit! Hit! Fight!' With that, John looked at Tiger, looked at the guard and then laid the guard out with one almighty punch! 'Ha!' exclaimed Tiger, beaming with pleasure, and went back to his office.

Over the Christmas period, Tiger had the prisoners construct a boxing ring. Still worried, L.B. John went to see the camp's interpreter and explained to him that he feared reprisals by the Korean guards while they were out at work. A little later, the interpreter reported back to John that Tiger had said there would be no reprisals. If there were, he personally would punish the guard responsible. Given the Tiger's blessing, on their next yasumi day, L.B. John laid out no less than eight of the guards in one afternoon. The Tiger was delighted and the prisoners felt quite happy about it, too.

New Year's Day 1943 was also a bonus yasumi day. The men in Bill's hut were all singing 'Auld Lang Syne' when toward the end of this traditional song, Tiger Hiramatsu and some Japanese officers entered the hut and applauded the prisoners' singing. 'All men, very good!' said Tiger repeatedly, smiling and clapping. The prisoners wondered what on earth he was clapping for as their singing hadn't exactly been heavenly, but just after they'd finished, Tiger started handing out biscuits to everyone. He seemed positively gleeful!

Not wishing to incur any sudden wrath for their non-comprehension of the situation, the prisoners just bowed Japanese style. Tiger and the officers seemed genuinely pleased by this, bowed in return and then left. Bill, among others, sought out the camp's interpreter and told him about it, after which he apparently just laughed. The interpreter then explained to Bill and his comrades that although he understood the men's customary singing of 'Auld Lang Syne', Tiger obviously didn't. The interpreter explained that the tune to 'Auld Lang Syne' is nearly the same as the Japanese national anthem! Tiger, not comprehending English too well, had obviously mistaken the tune and thought that the prisoners were saluting Japan, hence his obvious delight and rewarding of the men.

The interpreter thought the situation was quite humorous and did not bother to enlighten Tiger Hiramatsu, so the men in Bill's hut were able to hatch a ploy to play on the Tiger's kindly side further. At sunset, Bill explained, Tiger and some of the other Japanese were in the habit of going outside and praying to the setting sun. They'd all stand there chanting and bowing to the sun. Each line of their chant always seemed to end with the word 'osh'. A few of the prisoners used to go and stand behind them and mimic them, chanting: 'You are the cause of all this-osh. You are the cause of all this-osh', as they too, bowed repeatedly to the setting sun.

Once again it seems that Tiger Hiramatsu thought he was in charge of a group of model prisoners, and rewarded them with biscuits. The trouble was of course, that other prisoners soon cottoned-on to this scam and it wasn't long before there were sixty or so prisoners standing behind the Japanese, chanting. Inevitably, the biscuits ran out. With the sudden exhaustion of the biscuit supply, the men's apparent conversion to the Shinto religion proved to be remarkably short-lived.

One yasumi day, shortly after New Year, Bill and his comrades were out in the compound when one of his compatriots, 'Juddy' Edge, was suddenly called over by a Korean guard. Juddy went over to the guard and the rest of the men all worried what it was about. The guard engaged Juddy in some sort of conversation, which didn't look menacing at the time. Thinking that maybe the guard was carrying on some of the Christmas spirit that seemed present in the camp, the other prisoners relaxed a bit.

In fact, the guard was asking Juddy if he had a wife. Juddy said that he did. The guard then asked him if he had any children. Once again Juddy replied in the affirmative. 'Photo. You have photo-ka?' asked the smiling guard. Juddy did indeed have a rather battered photo of his family amongst his scant possessions. This is exactly what the guard was after.

Juddy produced the picture and gave it to the guard to look at. Suddenly, the guard's expression changed and he started laughing, except that it wasn't a kind laugh. The guard looked straight at Juddy then tore the photo up and shouted, 'No bruddy good!' as the pieces fell to the ground.

As Juddy bent down to retrieve the pieces, the sadistic guard

50

put his foot on them. Juddy straightened up and the guard, still laughing, then urinated on the torn photo. Bill and some of the other prisoners rushed over to restrain Juddy as they thought he might just murder the guard there and then, which would have been bad news for him. The Japanese would certainly have given Juddy a fearful bashing for it but Juddy seemed to be remarkably calm about the whole thing.

The reason Juddy hadn't responded to the guard's provocation, was that he could see past the guard's shoulder. A very angry-looking Tiger was fast coming up behind the guard, but the still laughing Korean was at that moment, blissfully ignorant of this fact.

But Tiger Hiramatsu had seen exactly what the guard had done and he did not approve. Tiger spun the surprised guard round and waded straight into him with a combination of the thick bamboo stick that he always carried, and his equally heavy fists. There was no stopping him, not that any of the prisoners particularly wanted to.

In a short space of time, Tiger Hiramatsu had reduced the guard's face to a barely recognizable, bloody pulp. Aiming one last kick at the now prostrated and bloodied guard, Tiger said vehemently, '*You* no bruddy good!' He then strode forcefully back to his office and slammed the door. The prisoners just went back to where they were before. Nobody bothered about the dazed and beaten guard; he was just left lying there.

Bill recalled that it was just after that little incident that the Japanese finally realized they'd previously been wasting a good two hours out of the twelve hours in their working day. The tool shed was at the bottom of the hill at Tonchan, by the landing stage where Bill had first arrived. Previously, the Japanese used to form everybody up for 'Tenko' (roll call), during which they'd be counted at least three times, then march all of them, which was the greater part of 2,000 men, down the hill to the tool shed. There they'd all be issued with the tools needed for that day's work before being marched back up the hill, through the main camp to work. Having suddenly realized this, the Japanese now moved the tool shed to the top of the hill.

With the surveying work complete, the specialists had been

put back with the other prisoners just before Christmas. Now that Christmas and New Year were over, they were assigned to carry out blasting work on what would soon become known as 'Hellfire Pass'.

Hellfire Pass was a cutting that had to be made through solid limestone rock. When finally completed, it was about 250 yards long, wide enough for a single-track railway about thirty feet deep, and had cost the lives of a good many men.

In preparation for the work at Hellfire Pass, a new camp called Tonchan South had been set up about six miles from the main camp, which was approximately halfway between Tonchan and Tarsao. They moved a lot of the men to this new camp. Squad Thompson, Jackie Boyce and Frank Steadman all went there and the specialists were sent to the new camp with them, though they were only there for a short while before being moved back to Tonchan main camp. Bill's group then seemed to flit between the two camps, so sometimes they had to walk twelve miles to work and sometimes it was only four, depending upon which camp they were at the night before.

Being two of the specialists, it fell to Bill and Cyril Hullcup to carry the explosives. The wooden box containing the sticks of gelignite weighed about twenty-seven pounds and Bill and Cyril had to carry it between them on the four-mile march to work from Tonchan South in the steamy heat of the jungle. Twenty-seven pounds may not sound like much in a book, but if you can imagine trying it for nearly two hours over rough terrain under extremely hot and humid conditions, when you've not eaten a decent meal for months and with a sadistic Korean guard behind you, who is only too willing to lay into you with a piece of bamboo if you so much as think of pausing, then perhaps the nature of the task involved becomes some-what clearer.

It was, in fact, under just those circumstances that a lot of the prisoners, Bill included, did get a 'bashing' merely for trying to inject a small amount of humour into their grim situation.

Bill remembered one particular morning, on the way to Hellfire Pass that Juddy Edge happened to look back at the line of men behind them. With all of them carrying picks, shovels, hammers or taps, it reminded him of the Gold Rush of 1849. Without warning, he suddenly shouted that they all looked like a load of forty-niners; that or gnomes.

There was a muffled laugh amongst the prisoners and then, as if taking his cue from this, Juddy burst into song. 'California, here we come!' is what he sang, and the rest of the prisoners joined in. This immediately incensed the guards, because they didn't allow any degree of happiness among the prisoners. The guards ran wildly among the men, indiscriminately hitting, slapping or whipping with their bamboo canes. 'All men no sing!' they shouted. 'All men march!' Such was the likely beginning to any working day on the Burma-Thailand railway.

It was about this time that some strange rumours reached the prisoners at Tonchan South. They began to hear all kinds of stories of a British counter-attack in Burma. Bill doesn't remember where those rumours came from, but after a while of hearing them, the men started to believe in them, even though there was absolutely no way of knowing whether the rumours were true or false.

So strongly did Bill come to believe in the rumours of the British regaining Burma, that he went to see the Battery Sergeant Major, Ben Pritchett, about it. It was all pure speculation on their part of course, but Bill bet Ben the sum of five pounds that they would all be free by August 1943. Pritchett was far from convinced by the rumours so the two men duly shook hands on it. Bill finally paid him those five pounds at a reunion, about fifty years later. Mind you, Bill really should have had an inkling that he'd have to pay Ben, when rumours went round the camp later that the Germans had finally managed to invade England. But the rumours were not altogether without foundation. The tide of the war was, in fact, already turning against the Japanese, but that fact had yet to be realized.

Being in the blasting party, it didn't take long for them to work out a technique for obtaining extra food. There were plenty of fish in the Kwai Noi but catching enough of them with just a homemade rod and line was a real problem. Time was also very much against them. So Sergeant Way, the Malay tin-mining engineer, worked out a way to steal some of the gelignite, so that they could blast the river for fish.

Way would deliberately over estimate the number of gelignite sticks needed for the job in hand. He would tell the Japanese that he would need, for example, six sticks of gelignite to do what they wanted. The Japanese guards didn't know, so they believed him, as they did know that Way was a mining engineer. Of course, the blasting party would then only use five sticks. It still made a big enough bang for the Japanese, and the prisoners would pocket the other stick.

They now had the explosive, but they still needed a means to detonate it underwater. To that end, Way told the Japanese that their fuse wire was practically useless for the job. Of course it wasn't, but the prisoners knew that the Japanese had a lot of British stuff they'd captured in Singapore. The British fuse wire was the only fuse wire that was known to burn underwater. A few carefully kinked or broken fuses were laid to demonstrate this 'flaw' in Japanese fuse wire. Not wishing to incur the wrath of their superiors for any untoward delays, the Japanese quickly procured some of the captured British fuse wire. Once they had it, it was really easy for the specialist prisoners to steal the required wire. The men laying the fuses just cut too much off the reel, laid what was needed, cut it again and concealed what they themselves needed to use.

But they thought they would have a harder time stealing an actual detonator. That was until Sergeant Way worked out a comically ingenious method for pinching one. Sergeant Way's method simply relied on the somewhat jittery nature of the Korean guards.

Each detonator had four metal claws on the end of it, to grip the fuse wire. Sergeant Way used to bite one of the claws over and tell the guards that because of this 'defect', the detonator just might malfunction and blow up in his face as he attached the fuse wire. The guards took him at his word and would back well away from him and turn their backs as he inserted the wire, just in case. Some would hide behind a rock or a tree for good measure. As he inserted the fuse wire, Way would shout 'Oh!' and the guards would cringe, waiting for the thing to go off!

While the guards weren't looking, Way would purloin another detonator from the open box.

All that was needed now was a means of collecting the hopefully masses of stunned fish once they'd blasted the river. It was while the conspirators were in their hut discussing this very point, that somebody just walked in, dropped a large green mosquito net on the floor, and walked out again, without saying a word.

A man quickly learned not to ask questions in the camps, as of course it was obvious that whoever had 'supplied' the net had broken into the Japanese stores and 'liberated' it. It was very much a case of what you didn't know, couldn't hurt you, or your partners in crime, for that matter. The men cut the mosquito net into a strip so that it was about thirty feet long and about seven feet deep, and then tied rocks and things into the bottom edge, to sink it. They now had the means to organize a 'fishing party'.

A fishing party would consist of about half a dozen prisoners. They would sneak out, as a group, after dark, as getting out of the camp was a lot easier than getting back in. The men would then carefully work their way to a point about a mile up river. Two or three men would then swim, with the net out, downstream from where the explosive would be thrown in and once the net was in position, Sergeant Way would insert the fuse wire into the detonator, light the fuse, and throw the charge into midstream.

As the charge detonated underwater, the noise was minimal and the stunned fish would float to the top and be carried downstream by the current, to the waiting net-men, who would frantically manoeuvre the net to catch as many of the fish as possible. The men each carried some fish in an improvised basket and made their way back to camp, separately. The fresh fish, secretly cleaned and gutted, were added to the rice stew that the prisoners were forced to live on. The fish guts were put in the latrine trenches. That way, nobody noticed the smell and the latrine's resident maggot population ate the evidence.

It was while returning from one of these late night fishing trips that the camp's sentries caught Bill, Andy Inglis and three others from a different fishing party. They were caught at different points as they emerged from the jungle. As usual, the other prisoners in the camp made a commotion to distract the guards, but it was already too late; they'd been seen. The men had already hidden the net and the fish, so they had nothing on them when they were caught, which is why the Japanese guards presumed that the prisoners were trying to escape. There was no point in the prisoners trying to convince the guards otherwise; they'd already made up their minds about it. Anything the prisoners said just met with a bashing.

The five men were taken into the middle of the camp and subjected to a savage beating by the guards, during which Bill's jaw was broken. Each man was then given a spade and told to dig a hole that was six feet long, three feet wide and six feet deep. The guards marked the holes out on the ground. One didn't have to be a genius to work out what the holes were for.

By the time the men had dug their own graves it was light. The other prisoners were roused by the guards and herded outside to where the five 'captured escapees' were all kneeling at the head of their graves. The Japanese always made an example of those prisoners they caught trying to escape. Bill and the four other men were to be that day's show.

Kneeling there in abject terror waiting for the end was, as Bill recounted, without doubt the worst moment of his entire life. As he was kneeling there, looking into his grave, he flinched as he heard a shot and one of the three from the other fishing party fell forward into his grave. Then another shot, and the man immediately to Bill's left tumbled forward. The guards were laughing all the time, a demented sort of laugh that sounded truly terrible; even maniacal. This was all a great joke to them. Then suddenly, Bill felt something very warm touch the back of his neck. He knew it was the barrel of the recently fired pistol.

As Bill knelt there, quaking with terror, he felt a pressure on his neck and heard a loud metallic 'click'. The next thing he heard was more demented laughter. Bill didn't know it, but the Gunsho (senior Japanese NCO) had unloaded his pistol after shooting the man next to him. They did exactly the same thing to Andy Inglis and the other fellow. The lucky three were then kicked forward into their graves, where the Japanese soldiers then urinated on each of them. The prisoners were then allowed to climb out and were made to fill in the two occupied graves before going back to their respective jobs of work on the railway. The other three graves were left open, as they were certain to be needed by the end of the day.

When Bill says that they were doing the blasting for the railway, it sounded like a fairly easy job when compared with the other prisoners' lot, but when he explained the nature of the work involved, it became apparent that it was anything but easy.

The accident rate among the prisoners was quite high. Although the prisoners were all undernourished and most of them were sick with malaria or dysentery (or both), or some other equally debilitating tropical disease, a man had to literally be at death's door before the Japanese would even consider excusing him from work. For example, a broken arm would only get a man two days off in the hospital and lighter duties for a week; then he was put back on regular work detail.

When blasting, Bill's group used to start with the setting out of eighteen holes, in a very long line. (No, they weren't about to play some bizarre form of golf!) The holes were the boreholes down which the explosives would be placed, in order to create a fissure in the limestone rock. The holes had to be made with a hammer and tap, that is a sledgehammer and a three-foot long cold chisel. There was also a 'bucket man' at each hole with his bucket of water.

One man would sit on the rock holding the cold chisel, whilst his 'oppo' would wield the sledgehammer. After each strike of the hammer, the tap man had to twist the chisel in order to make any progress downward. The bucket man would have to pour water down the hole to turn the dust and loose chippings into a paste that would stick to the chisel. That was the only way to clear the hole ready for the gelignite charges. All this would have to be done under a blazing sun that not only heated the surface of the rock they were sitting or standing on, but also beat down mercilessly onto their heads and the already sunburnt skin of their emaciated bodies. Most of the men by that time were reduced to wearing nothing but a shabby loincloth which they called a 'Jap-happy', as the clothes that they'd been captured in had long ago rotted away. The Japanese never gave them any new clothes.

Once, when Bill was the tap man and Sergeant Way was wielding the hammer, he had an accident. Both men were sick with malaria. Shivering feverishly as their body temperatures hovered at about 105 degrees, and with the hot sun beating down on them, Sergeant Way mis-hit the chisel Bill was holding for him. The sledgehammer glanced off the chisel head and hit Bill's left shin. He screamed out and looked down at the wound. Because his skin was so thin from malnutrition, the hammer had split it right to the bone. Bill still has a sizeable scar from it, even now.

One of the guards hurried over, shouting 'Nando?' meaning why had they stopped working without permission. Bill pointed to his shin and said 'Dame dana' which roughly translated means 'it's bad' and given that you could actually see the bone, Bill thought it was bad. But the guard's opinion was different. 'Nai. Not dame dana. Fit. All men fit. All men work.' he snapped. Bill wrapped a piece of rag round his shin and carried on. He'd not long recovered from the broken jaw and had no wish for further breakages. He went to see the MO later, after work and he cleaned the wound and dressed it a little better, but it was still extremely painful, especially at work.

Bill also recalls that the warped sense of humour the Japanese possessed could manifest itself at any time at work. He remembers one particular day during the blasting for Hellfire Pass, when he, Sergeant Way and Juddy Edge had set out and bored the eighteen holes and put the charges into them, and were in the process of setting the fuses when, on a whim, a Japanese engineer came along and made some changes behind their backs.

Usually, Sergeant Way put short fuses on the middle six holes and longer ones on the two outside groups of six, so as to give them time to get clear. But this day, the Japanese engineer changed the fuses around and lit all of them while the three men were still working in the middle. They heard a shout, looked round and saw the burning fuses. The three now had to run about 150 yards across either of the outside set of fuses to safety, with the short fuses on both sets of the outside six charges fast approaching the point of detonation.

In their haste to get clear, the men left their buckets behind. There was the usual big bang and the force of the explosion knocked the three prisoners off their feet. The next thing they knew, it seemed to be raining buckets.

As the three men finally scrambled clear of the blasting area, the Japanese engineer, who had prematurely lit the fuses, tore into them. He had nearly been hit by one of the descending buckets, all of which were now, of course, completely ruined. The three men then got a summary bashing for damaging Japanese Army equipment!

Before Hellfire Pass was completed, the rains came. The monsoon season had arrived slightly early in April 1943 but, rain or shine, work on the Emperor's railway continued. If the blazing sun were beating down on them, the Japanese always stood in the shade. When it rained, the Japanese wore oilskin capes over their uniforms. The prisoners were never issued with anything to shade them or keep them dry.

What nobody there at the time knew, not even the Japanese, was that with the annual monsoon rains came a deadly scourge every year to Thailand; cholera. To the already weak and sick prisoners, this was to prove devastating.

The camp already had men sick with dysentery, malaria and beriberi. Some of the worst cases at that time were those with cerebral malaria. Those poor devils had convulsive screaming fits as well as the usual symptoms and hardly any of them survived. Beriberi caused a man swell up with water, particularly in the neck, abdomen and 'nether regions'. It was extremely painful and it, too, could be fatal, but cholera would prove far worse than any disease the prisoners had yet encountered.

Death was no stranger to the prisoners held in the railway camps. It visited them every single day and every single night. For some, it was undoubtedly a merciful release, but it always hit harder if it was somebody that you had known before, rather than someone you'd met in the camp. Bill remembers being told one day that Frank Steadman was ill in the hospital hut. Naturally, he went to see him after work. The poor man had both dysentery and malaria, which wasn't a good combination.

He looked absolutely awful. All the men looked awful anyway, but Frank looked particularly bad to Bill.

Bill spent some time trying to comfort his friend in the grim surroundings. Suddenly, Frank looked at him and said: 'I don't want to die yet Bill, I really don't.' Bill told him that he was talking nonsense; that there was no way he was going to die. Then after a little while longer, Bill left him. The next day, Squad and Jackie managed to pass word to Bill at work that Frank had died during the night. Bill felt anger such as he had never really known up to then. In Bill's mind, there was simply no need for it to have happened. There was no need for any of the suffering, the degradation, the deprivation or the awful conditions. It was solely because of those 'little yellow bastards' as Bill still calls them, who worshipped Hirohito.

On one of the last working parties before the cholera epidemic swept through the camp, Bill witnessed another Japanese atrocity. They were returning to camp in the driving rain when one of the men who was already being helped along by his mates, suddenly collapsed. His mates shouted for a stretcher, which would have been two rice sacks with two bamboo poles shoved through them, when a Japanese NCO pushed through the small crowd to look at the collapsed and now unconscious man on the floor. 'Engerish prisoner no good, no work no more.' he said. With that, the Japanese soldier took out a perang, which was a large and very sharp knife for cutting bamboo, and struck the collapsed prisoner right across the face with it, twice, splitting his skull.

The other prisoners went to pick up their fallen comrade's body, but the Japanese NCO prevented them from doing so and moved the men on. They marched back to camp, but later on Bill found out that a couple of the dead man's comrades sneaked out of camp and buried him in the jungle that night. That was just one more example of the Japanese at work. Then the cholera came.

Cholera is a water-borne disease. Highly contagious, it starts with extremely painful stomach cramps. Then comes fever, with intense vomiting and diarrhoea and if left untreated, death will usually occur within twelve to eighteen hours of the first signs.

The treatment varied, but the main enemy was total dehydration, which lead to kidney failure. The medics in the camps tried their hardest, some even making makeshift saline 'drips' from empty bottles, rubber hoses and bamboo thorns. Some miracles were achieved, but by and large, the men died in agony by the hundreds as the cholera epidemic took hold.

The Japanese were mightily afraid of cholera and with good reason. Cholera didn't care who it killed. Prisoners died at work, in their crude huts or in the hospital huts. The Japanese barricaded their own quarters and only came out wearing masks. In the meantime, work on the railway stopped and those prisoners still able to walk built huge fires to burn the bodies of the dead. It was absolutely appalling. The men kept those fires burning day and night, for days. There were so many of them that died that the Japanese had to call upon civilian labour, as well as more prisoners from Singapore and Burma, to work on the railway.

The Japanese brought in Tamils, Javanese and Chinese labourers. Told that the Japanese Army would provide free transport, free accommodation and would pay them a wage, these civilians, many of them entire families including children, volunteered to work on the railway. Upon arrival at the camps, they were more than dismayed to find themselves living and working under exactly the same harsh conditions as the prisoners of war.

The civilians came up to Tonchan towards the end of the cholera epidemic. The trouble was, the disease was still rife in the camp. Their sanitary methods were not the same as those of the prisoners. Whereas the prisoners of war at least dug latrine trenches, which the Japanese for some absurd reason never let them fill in once they were full, most of the civilian labourers just defecated anywhere. Not surprisingly, they were nearly all wiped out by the cholera shortly after they arrived.

As the rains stopped and the cholera slowly died out, those prisoners who had survived were given the task of clearing the corpses of the cholera victims out of the civilian camp. There were a few of the civilians who'd survived too, and the prisoners actually found out from them that there was a certain tree indigenous to the Thai jungle whose bark contained quinine, the magical remedy for the symptoms of malaria. The downside of this was that the bark tasted absolutely awful as it was chewed and although it certainly worked, this raw quinine had a stupefying effect, so although the malarial symptoms were relieved, the likelihood of a bashing from the guards, over the sloth-like performance of a task, was greatly increased. The secret, therefore, lay in chewing just enough of the bark as was necessary to take the edge off the malarial symptoms and make the condition almost bearable while at work.

With the passing of the cholera epidemic, the Japanese now found that the construction of the Emperor's railway was way behind their schedule. More prisoners were brought up from Singapore, more civilian labour was drafted in and the saga of the Railway of Death entered its most terrible chapter. It became known as the 'Speedo' period.

Chapter Six

'SPEEDO!'

With the railway so far behind schedule, the Japanese now ruthlessly weeded out any causes of delay that they could find. British officers, with their 'bulldog spirit' and their 'stiff upper lip', stubbornly standing up for their men or constantly protesting about the conditions or treatment, used up precious time, even if it was only the time needed to hear that officer's words via an interpreter and then administer the inevitable savage beating for his 'insubordination'. No officers, no complaints; that was how the Japanese now viewed the situation. The officers were all moved to the camp at Kanchanaburi. There they elected the charismatic Colonel Toosey to be the senior British officer, even though there were other colonels present who were far more senior.

Colonel Toosey was one of those rare men that always seemed to know the right thing to say or do, even though his words and deeds frequently earned him a bashing from the Japanese or worse, incarceration in the 'no-good house', an unbelievably tiny cell in which a man could neither stand nor lie down, located in full sun and with a corrugated metal roof. Toosey's leadership of the imprisoned officers was nothing short of inspirational and it is lamentable that he was quite wrongly portrayed as a collaborator by Alec Guinness' character in the film *Bridge on the River Kwai*.

Toosey was anything but a collaborator. In the film, he is portrayed as being determined to prove to the Japanese that the British had the engineering expertise that they apparently lacked, which is why their railway was behind schedule. In return for something like proper treatment, the Colonel would get the prisoners to build an outstanding timber bridge for the Japanese, on time.

Nothing could have been further from the truth. The main bridge at Tamarkan was not made from timber at all. Although a temporary timber bridge was built there, its purpose was secondary. It is worth pointing out that the bridge at Tamarkan does not cross the Kwai Noi anyway. It crosses a tributary of the main river called the Kwai Yai. Furthermore, there is no 'River Kwai'. Kwai means 'river' in Thai. Kwai Noi is in fact the Noi River. (Kwai Yai incidentally, means Little River.) Therefore, a more accurate title for the film would have been 'Bridge on the Little River' but the film's director apparently liked the sound of the word 'Kwai' so he effectively called his film, which is far from being an accurate account, 'Bridge on the River River'.

The Japanese were certainly not lacking in engineering expertise. They had already cleverly adapted several diesel lorries to run on standard gauge railway track. These lorries were even able to pull two or sometimes three railway trucks, or up to seven makeshift flat-cars, and were a great help to the Japanese as temporary trains, hauling timber and work gangs along the completed parts of the line during the railway's construction.

In fact, the Burma-Thailand railway was arguably one of the finest engineering feats of the Second World War. But that statement needs to be very carefully balanced by the knowledge of the 100,000 lives that were mercilessly sacrificed in its construction.

What Toosey in reality proved, to his own men as well as the Japanese, was that they could stand up to every deprivation, every torment and every bit of suffering that the Japanese could inflict upon them and still maintain discipline, courage and above all, that indomitable British spirit. History, unlike the film, shows that Colonel Toosey was entirely successful in achieving that aim.

The first sign that the rank and file prisoners had that things had changed was, of course, this sudden removal of all their officers. There were no explanations. The most senior man that was left to the prisoners after that was Bill's Battery Sergeant Major, Ben Pritchett.

Another measure that was introduced, once the officers had been removed, was the 'simplification' of the working day and yasumi days. Henceforth, the prisoners' working day was divided into two twelve-hour shifts as the Japanese introduced round-the-clock working on the railway, and yasumi days were now limited to just one per month. With the population of the camps decimated by the recent cholera epidemic, more labour, prisoners and civilian, was brought up from Singapore and anywhere else that the Japanese could find workers.

As work on the railway resumed, 'Speedo' turned from being a shouted command into a way of life. Sadistic guards, already used to driving sick and exhausted prisoners to their very limits, now set about their frenzied slave driving with renewed vigour. In fact, most of them performed the task with relish.

The trouble with the Korean guards was quite simply due to the fact that the Japanese hated them almost as much as they detested the prisoners. The Koreans too were a conquered people and these guards were conscripted into the Japanese Army. The conscripts had no status, no chance of promotion and no recognition from their Japanese superiors. The Japanese persecuted the Koreans, who in turn persecuted the prisoners, with zeal.

Yet not all of the Korean guards were so inclined. Bill and quite a few other prisoners got an unexpected shock one day when an unusually tall and well-muscled Korean guard quietly entered their hut. Dropping two dead chickens on the nearest bed, the big Korean introduced himself as 'American Joe'.

At first, the prisoners naturally distrusted the man. But Joe quickly gained their trust by sneaking much-needed food to them. Had Joe been discovered in this, his Japanese masters would undoubtedly have tortured and executed him. The prisoners soon realized that they had an unexpected friend and it wasn't long before the prisoners naturally asked 'Big Joe' as they preferred to call him due to his being over six feet tall, why he was running such risks on their behalf.

Joe, it transpired, was a Christian. The Japanese had shot both of his parents when they conquered his country and Joe had been conscripted into the Japanese Army. Furthermore, Joe's two younger sisters, of whom he was extremely fond, had been taken away by the Japanese and were now serving the Emperor as 'comfort girls' to Japanese officers. In other words, Joe had been forced to serve in the very army that had murdered his parents and enslaved his sisters into a life of forced prostitution. Big Joe understandably had no love for the Japanese and consequently, he did his utmost to help the prisoners in any way that he was able.

By the time the 'Speedo' really got under way, Bill and his group had almost finished the blasting work for Hellfire Pass. Once the rock had been blasted, teams of prisoners using sledgehammers further reduced the limestone. The much-reduced rock was then ferried out of the cutting by a constant stream of prisoners using baskets on a yoke or something like a stretcher. These rocks were utilized as the foundation of an embankment at one end of the pass. While the other men were driven like demons to clear away the rocks, the specialists were moved to the site of Wampo viaduct, to lend a hand with the blasting for that part of the project. Just before they left for Wampo, Bill witnessed another example of the prisoners' expendability, as an Australian trooper was purposefully buried alive under tons of the rock that Bill and his comrades had blasted.

This particular Aussie trooper was carrying two baskets of rocks suspended on a shoulder-mounted yoke, when he finally collapsed under his burden and fell down the embankment. Seeing the man fall, the other prisoners in the line put their loads down and were going to their fallen comrade's aid when some Japanese guards prevented them. Pointing to the fallen prisoner, a Japanese sergeant bellowed: 'This man no fit! This man dame dana! All fit men work!' The prisoners were made to pick up their loads and carry on depositing the rocks onto the embankment foundation, of which the Australian, as far as that Japanese sergeant was concerned, had just become an integral part.

Wampo viaduct was back down the line from Hellfire Pass and was to be built on a ledge running round one side of a mountain. It was the task of the blasting parties to create that ledge. When finished, the viaduct was a most impressive tiered wooden trestle that was built along the same design lines as the huge trestle bridges on the American Trans-Continental Railroad. This was hardly surprising, as the Japanese engineers were working from the very manual that the American engineers had used to construct their great 2,000-mile railroad that stretched all the way across the United States.

But the Japanese use of the American 'Merriman Manual' of civil engineering meant that the Burma-Thailand railway was extremely over-engineered when it came to bridges and viaducts. The impressively huge and immensely strong trestles in America were designed to carry much bigger, heavier locomotives and trains than would ever be used on the Japanese railway. This meant that the bridges and viaducts on the Burma-Thailand railway were built far stronger than they needed to be and building the railway to such an over-specification meant a corresponding over-strain on the labourers who were already being driven harder than galley slaves. Not that the Japanese cared either way. If the labour of their captives was cheap, their lives were even more so.

The great trestle viaduct at Wampo, as originally constructed, carried the Burma-Thailand railway line at a height of almost 200 feet as it climbed toward Hellfire Pass. The fact that it is still in use today, though somewhat diminished in height and with a painfully slow speed restriction imposed on the diesel trains that still rumble across it, bears testament to the extraordinary men who were forced to build it by hand out of blood, sweat, timber and tears and from many hundreds of whom the Japanese glee-fully and relentlessly extracted the ultimate price for their labours.

By this time, the wound on Bill's leg that Sergeant Way accidentally gave him with his sledgehammer had truly begun to fester. Not only was the shinbone plainly visible, but also the flesh around the original tear had ulcerated and the hole was getting noticeably bigger by the day. Bill protested to one of the more senior guards and showed him the wound. He was told that he still had one good leg to stand on to wield a hammer, or he could sit down to hold a tap. Either way, he was not excused from a work detail. From now on, everybody was to be sacrificed to the construction of the Emperor's railway.

To truly illustrate a typical day on the railway during the 'Speedo' period would be impossible, as mere words simply could not convey its sheer horror. For prisoners on the day shift, the day usually started amid the chill wisps of the dawn mist that floated on the Kwai Noi. This was at about 06:00. A harsh Japanese bugle-call would reverberate around the camp, summoning the dishevelled and emaciated prisoners to the cookhouse hut, there to queue for a mug of foul, stodgy rice; such was breakfast. If the men were lucky, there might just be time for a quick wash, without the luxury of soap, in the river before tenko. Teeth cleaning, grooming and shaving were by that time but a distant memory.

After the invariable thrice counting at tenko, the men would return to the cookhouse to collect another mug of rice. This would be their midday meal, provided that the jungle ants didn't beat them to it, although the rice would turn sour in the heat by midday anyway. After collecting this second mug, the men would proceed to the tool shed to collect their tools. Then the column would march or limp off to work.

Soon, the unbearably humid jungle air would be filled with the sounds of trees being felled, bamboo being cut, sledgehammers striking the taps, or picks and shovels scraping away at the rocky subsoil. Depending upon which section of the line one was at, the noise of blasting would punctuate the other sounds and the very air would reverberate with the shock waves. Teams of near naked, half-dead and constantly hungry prisoners hauled, dug, clawed or hammered in the merciless heat of the Thai jungle, clearing the way or laying the sleepers.

Those building the smaller bridges worked at piledriving, using an entirely manual process. A large timber frame suspended the heavy log used as the piledriver. Ropes ran through a pulley above this frame and teams of men literally hauled in unison on these ropes, raising the piledriver high above the sharpened tree trunk that was to be the upright for the bridge frame.

Working to a Japanese counting rhythm with blistered, friction-burnt hands, the teams hauled and let go, hauled and let go, as the heavy log repeatedly crashed down onto the timber upright until the Japanese engineer was satisfied that the upright

68

had been driven in to a sufficient depth. Then the upright would be cut to the correct level in-situ. There is hardly a man who survived the railway camps that doesn't still recall 'Ici, Ni, San, Shi, Go!' without trepidation.

Those men set to work on building embankments, such as the sixty feet high and 400 yard long embankment at Kinsaioke, had to excavate the soil required by hand, carry it in twenty pound basket-loads up the steep, ever increasing slope that they were building, deposit the load at the top and then work their way down again to repeat the seemingly endless process. As always, there was the shouted command of 'Speedo' accompanied by a blow from a bamboo stick to cure the prisoner's apparent lethargy.

The prisoners soon came to appreciate the seemingly endless versatility of bamboo. They used lengths of it as rollers to move heavy loads, they built huts and even small bridges with it, fashioned eating utensils from it, slept on beds made from it, drank rainwater from the thick hollow bottom of it, made tables and stools out of it, cut themselves on its vicious thorns, were beaten daily with it and finally had their last resting place in the Thai jungle marked with it.

By late morning, the fierce tropical sun would begin to take its steady toll on the emaciated workforce. Men would start to wilt, then collapse. As soon as a man passed out he would instantly be pounced on by a guard and viciously beaten with a bamboo stick or the guard's rifle butt, always to shouts of 'Nai! You work! Up! Speedo! Speedo!' until he either got up and resumed work or he moved no more.

Even the sick, who were unable to stand or walk, were taken out of the hospital huts and carried by their less sick comrades to work on stretchers. Once at work, the stretcher cases would be placed in the semi-shade with a small hammer, a chisel and a never-ending supply of large stones, which they had to break up to make ballast for the track. Any prisoner too sick to fill his quota wouldn't last the day anyway.

Anyone who earnestly pleaded 'benjo' (toilet) would be scrutinized by the guards as he disappeared into the undergrowth with a handful of soft leaves. If he didn't re-emerge quickly enough and with his own personal following of flies, the guards would find him and kick him back to work.

At midday a whistle would blow, followed by the welcome shout of: 'All work stop! All men Meishi!' The prisoners were then allowed the luxury of a twenty-minute lunch break; time to consume their second mug of now cold, sour and ant-infested rice. At first, some tried to evict the raiding ants but soon, most prisoners just stirred them into the rice and ate it anyway. Perhaps the ants had some nutritional value, which is certainly more than the rice had. Exactly twenty minutes after they'd stopped for lunch, another whistle announced that it was time to go back to work. Those who lingered for as long as two seconds after the guard's whistle sounded were flogged into action for their tardiness.

So the agonizing day wore on. More beatings, more deaths, more jungle cleared, more piles driven, more trees felled, more rocks broken, more earth moved and more track laid. Eventually, the rapid dusk of the Thai jungle came. The sky turned to vivid shades of red, gold and purple as the sun quickly disappeared below the tropical tree-filled skyline and daylight gave way to the star-filled indigo heavens. Not that anyone noticed such a beautiful scene any more, belying as it did, the hellish misery being suffered below.

About an hour before dusk came, the relief column arrived of those who would carry on with the punishing work schedule. Night work on the Emperor's railway continued under the glare of flame torches as a fresh batch of living skeletons toiled through the darkness, re-enacting the whole panoply of miserable scenes previously played out by the day shift skeletons. They, having now buried those of their number who had succumbed to the ravages of another day, trudged zombie-like back to camp, there to consume another meagre meal before finally falling onto their hard bamboo-slat beds to rest for a few hours, before starting the whole gruelling process again the following morning.

Day and night quickly grew meaningless and the weeks and months simply blurred into one interminable nightmare, always with the men being beaten, flogged and driven to the point of collapse with guttural shouts of 'Speedo' as a continual accompaniment. Such was life, work and death for the prisoners of the Japanese.

As the crude bamboo crosses steadily multiplied in the jungle and the hospital huts filled with dying men, so the Japanese demands for increased efforts grew. His superiors now issued Tiger Hiramatsu, the enigmatic commandant of Tonchan camp, with daily quotas for the number of men that his camp was required to supply for the Railway Regiment's work details. Tiger soon found himself unable to meet those quotas; he simply hadn't sufficient numbers of remotely fit men in the camp. He was told to find them; failure wasn't an option. Tiger Hiramatsu knew only too well what the price of failure was in the Imperial Japanese Army.

In an effort to secure more workers, Tiger raided the camp's hospital huts. From now on he decreed that only prisoners who were physically incapable of standing would be excused from work. The British medical officer protested loudly at this and fifteen minutes later was himself being treated by his own orderlies for the injuries he received from the guards as Hiramatsu left the hut.

Unbeknown to the prisoners at that time however, was the fact that Tiger Hiramatsu was now fighting a bitter conflict within himself, trying hard to reconcile the unquestioning obedience and loyalty that his superiors demanded of him, with the strict and honourable doctrines of his religious beliefs. As the 'Speedo' period progressed, he began to realize that the two were in fact quite irreconcilable. He grew increasingly morose and perhaps inevitably, he sought solace inside a Thai whiskey bottle, which only served to make him ever more foul-tempered and unapproachable.

As Tiger withdrew into himself, the excesses committed by the guards against the prisoners grew more frequent and more diabolical. It was no longer enough for their sadistic appetites simply to work or beat a man to death. Now, the guards turned to torture as well, for the slightest misdemeanour and sometimes purely for sport.

For 'slacking' at work, a prisoner was usually made to stand on a rock facing the sun while holding either another rock or a pickaxe high above his head. He would also have to stare open-eyed at the sun for the duration of his ordeal. The prisoner was left there, strictly guarded, until he collapsed. A prisoner who was caught stealing food was tied to a tree with barbed wire and left for three days without food, but with a bucket of fresh water placed in front of him, just out of his reach. For 'insubordination' the punishment varied from an instant beating to being strung up by the thumbs so that the prisoner's toes only just touched the ground, and being left like that all day.

The favourite 'sporting torture' of the guards was to tie a prisoner's hands behind his back with barbed wire and lay him down on the ground. Then while four guards held him down, a rubber hose was forced down his throat into his stomach. The guards would then pour as much water into his stomach as they could funnel through the hose. When the prisoner's distended abdomen could hold no more water, the hose was withdrawn and the guards would then take it in turns to jump, laughing, feet first onto the prisoner's belly. They would often take bets amongst themselves as to how long the prisoner would last before either vomiting the water back, or suffering a ruptured stomach. In any event, the game always resulted in either the prisoner's death or the destruction of his stomach muscles. Bill recalled that sometimes, the guard who'd lost the bet would take it out on the prisoner by bayoneting his water-filled stomach. He'd seen that happen quite a few times. When they played that game with Bill, he was lucky. The losing guard just accepted his loss of the bet and contented himself with giving Bill a parting kick as he left. After a short while, Bill was released.

Soon, more tools and equipment arrived by barge. Rails came up to be laid, brought up by heavy lorries on dirt roads through the jungle. The Japanese dismantled other, less important railways in their newly conquered territories in order to save time and money. Tamarkan Bridge, the concrete and steel structure which we encountered earlier, was in fact dismantled at its original location on a railway in Java and brought over in sections to Thailand, where it was painfully reconstructed by hand, without the benefit of any heavy machinery, in its present location. Like Wampo viaduct, the bridge is still in use today.

Bill and the other specialists were ultimately spared death from the punishing work schedule of the 'Speedo' period when the Japanese decided to utilize their skills once more. They were handed over to a Japanese engineer who, with the aid of a Welshman who, of course, was called Taffy, trained them all to be blacksmiths. They first had to build a forge and their own sleeping quarters behind it, but as soon as they'd made themselves as comfortable as was possible, they were assigned to their new task. A lorry-load of old packing tools was delivered to them and the newly-qualified 'blacksmiths' turned them into 3,000 pecks, which were hand tools used to spread and bank the ballast gravel under and around the wooden sleepers of the railway track.

Bill's time as a blacksmith was cut short however, due to his now badly ulcerated leg. By now, the flesh was truly rotting and a three-inch section of his shinbone was showing. In September 1943, Bill was finally moved to the hospital unit in Tarsao camp, for treatment. The hospital unit was separate from the main camp and sited right beside the river. One of the others already in the hospital there, Bill discovered, was Juddy Edge.

Bill wondered what treatment he would receive. He'd seen some ghastly treatments for ulcers at Tonchan and he wasn't looking forward to it at all. However, Bill was in luck, as were almost all the patients there, due to the presence of two extraordinary men. The first was an Australian soldier who had previously been a sheep farmer. The second was a local man named Bhoon Pong.

Bhoon Pong owned one of the supply barges that regularly plied the river. Appalled by what he saw going on in the camps, he did his best to help the prisoners. In what must surely rate as the most trusting, unorthodox and astounding business transaction ever, Bhoon Pong accepted a cheque from the Australian soldier/sheep farmer for $250,000, which he was told not to cash till after the war. In return, Bhoon Pong smuggled precious and urgently needed medical supplies into the camp hospital on a twice-weekly basis for the remainder of the war. A good many men certainly owe their limbs, if not their lives to this amazing arrangement.

After a few weeks of almost proper treatment, Bill's ulcerated leg had healed sufficiently for him to be classified as 'light sick'. He and Juddy Edge teamed up with another patient called Jimmy Bartlett, who was a cockney lad from Poplar in east London and the three of them took to stealing supplies from the barges they unloaded, for distribution amongst their fellow prisoners in Tarsao camp. Priority in the issuing of these stolen supplies was always given to those in the hospital unit, particularly salt and peanuts.

One day, a familiar friend arrived in the shape of the guard Big Joe. He'd been transferred to Tarsao from Tonchan, purely due to the usual rotation and movements of the guards. Joe was fortuitously assigned to oversee and guard those prisoners unloading the supply barges. As well as making his 'snap hut inspections' which were, of course, nothing more than his customary 'supply drops' of sweet potatoes and the odd chicken, Big Joe helpfully tipped Bill, Juddy and Jimmy off to the fact that the little wild pigs that were sent by barge as fresh meat supplies for the Japanese officers, couldn't swim. Joe would always make sure that the other guards were diverted while Bill or another of the three ensured that at least one pig swiftly drowned during the unloading operation and that the carcass was spirited away.

There was another source of food for the prisoners that came from an unexpected source. Although it proved to be a 'one-off', it was most welcome at the time.

Having returned from a day spent unloading the barges, Bill was standing with Juddy and Jimmy in the long line for the cook-house, anticipating nothing more mouth-watering than the usual mug of foul rice when a passing prisoner quietly whispered to them that they were to collect their rice and casually follow him. There was, they were assured, 'something else on the menu'. The three duly did as they were instructed and much to their delight, they were each given a decent sized portion of meat to go with their rice. Furthermore, the meat was still warm from cooking.

Having consumed their meal, the men naturally wanted to

know the nature of the unusually sweet-flavoured meat that they'd so enjoyed, so they sought out the man who'd told them about it. 'Can't say right now,' he told them, 'but you'll soon know when a certain Jap can't find what he's looking for!' Mystified, the three men went back to their hut to rest. The penny dropped later, when the camp Commandant was seen anxiously looking everywhere for his white bulldog, who for some reason seemed to have disappeared! The Commandant's anxiety was further heightened when he discovered that his pony had also vanished without trace the same day. It would seem that the camp's Australian contingent had also eaten well that evening!

'The three racketeers' also decided to start up their own business as tobacconists. Bill sold his Royal Artillery cap to a local trader for $5.00. With that $5.00, he bought an 18oz block of tobacco from one of the supply boat traders. Using the pages of a bible that one of the other two had acquired, the three started making cigarettes. If they were careful, they could get eight to ten 'ciggies' out of one page of the bible. They used to put sixteen of these 'economically produced' cigarettes into one of the many Oxo tins that were to be found in amongst every prisoner's possessions and they could get forty tins out of the 18oz block. The tins of sixteen were then sold to the other prisoners. The currency was either the local coin, called a tical, or the wage tokens issued by the Japanese. The local traders accepted either. The empty tins were always returned to Bill for refilling and their 'brand' became known as 'Old Testaments' due to the biblical nature of the rolling paper!

Another good money-spinner was burnt rice coffee. Jimmy Bartlett put them onto that one. The burnt rice came from the cookhouse bins and they used to scrape it out surreptitiously. It was then sweetened with Gualala Malacca, which is not unlike black treacle that was stolen from the barges. Hot water was then added to the two ingredients and the resultant brew sold at fifty cents a mug.

The three racketeers soon amassed a sizable amount of the ten-cent wage tokens issued by the Japanese. Ten cents was the daily rate of pay for an ordinary soldier. Specialists such as Bill and Juddy received fifteen cents a day. One small banana from a local trader typically cost seventy cents. A small jar of Marmite or Bovril, a godsend to the hospital patients as a source of badly needed vitamins, cost a king's ransom when they could get it.

During Bill's time in the hospital at Tarsao, the construction of the railway had progressed at a remarkable rate. As the track had been laid, Bill and the other prisoners suddenly began to see more and more of the Japanese Railway Regiment's soldiers in Tarsao. The Japanese men of these regiments appeared to be different and were pretty much a law unto themselves. There was one particular Japanese officer in the 9 Railway Regiment at Tarsao who soon proved to be every inch a thorough sadist. His name, Bill says, was Sugano.

If this young officer had one passion in his life it apparently was trains. He was quite a keen amateur photographer too and liked nothing better than to combine these interests, but the trains were definitely his first love. He'd come up with the first engines that arrived because Tarsao was in fact a depot for the railway; there were sidings and a large fuel store there. His only concern was to get the trains through to Burma as quickly as possible. Ardent and utterly ruthless, he would allow nothing and no one to stand in the way of his dream of the early completion of the Emperor's railway. He extensively photographed scenes of the railway under construction, but he was careful not to show the suffering of the prisoners in his charge in any detail. Bill is of the opinion that if this particular Japanese officer had been born a German, he would have made a first-rate Nazi.

Among the prisoners, Sugano quickly acquired a reputation as a slave driver par excellence. One day, this young officer set a grisly, stage-managed example to all, of what would happen to those who, in his opinion, tried to frustrate his glorious dream.

That day is one that Bill will never forget. The prisoners, including Bill and Juddy Edge, were all called up to the sidings that morning where Sugano was standing beside the track. He announced to the assembled prisoners that one of their number had been caught trying to escape the previous night. Bill says this was patently untrue as by that time everyone was far too weak to attempt escape. The man in question had undoubtedly been out foraging for food and was in all likelihood caught trying to sneak back in again.

However, according to Sugano's reasoning, (if one could call it that) by trying to 'escape' the prisoner was apparently attempting to deprive the Emperor of his labour effort. This was therefore stealing and of course, everyone knew the penalties likely to be suffered for that.

Bill recalls that as Sugano came to end of his little speech, a locomotive came puffing up the line. Tied across its front buffers was the captured 'escapee', a man from the Sherwood Foresters Regiment. The approaching loco was switched into the sidings and halted next to Sugano, in front of the assembled prisoners, who were then made to watch as, in Sugano's own words, the prisoner, whom it was obvious had already received a severe beating, now 'paid for his crime'. Bill says that at Sugano's signal to the engine driver, exhaust steam gushed from the locomotive's cylinders and it moved slowly forward with its living human buffers, and commenced shunting work in the sidings.

At the beginning of November 1943, the Japanese swept through the hospital units of most camps looking for remotely fit men. Nearing discharge and classified as only 'light sick' Bill, Juddy Edge and Jimmy Bartlett were among those selected from Tarsao. Bill and Jimmy Bartlett were sent up to Three Pagodas Pass, where the railway crossed the Thailand-Burma border. Juddy Edge was sent south.

Everyone's favourite guard, Big Joe, was also routinely transferred during this movement. He was sent south to the officers' camp at Kanchanaburi. Bill never saw him or Juddy again.

Bill's party went north by train, on the railway they had built. Among the others going north, Bill discovered his old mate Dickey Francis. They were astonished to find that the railway had in fact been completed about five weeks previously. Given that situation, the men wondered what horrors the Japanese had planned for them now that the 'Speedo' was so obviously over. They didn't have to wait long to find out.

Chapter Seven

LOGS AND DUCKS

The Emperor's railway was now complete, but the trains using the new line to transport Japanese troops, equipment and ammunition through the 'back door' into Burma, needed fuel. As there was no coal in Thailand, the engines had to burn wood, tons of it in fact. Bill and his comrades were about to become lumberjacks for the Imperial Japanese Army.

They were not the first to arrive at Three Pagodas Pass and as soon as they'd disentrained, they went straight to the camp. Bill almost walked straight into Squad Thompson, who was already there. The Japanese also brought up bamboo on the train, for the prisoners to build their huts.

Once they'd built their huts, the men were divided into groups of six. Bill was with Squad, Jimmy Bartlett, a chap called Danny Pinnock, another chap called Washbrook and someone else whose name escapes Bill now. These groups of six were then taken out into the jungle, always close to the railway at first, and each man had to cut logs averaging eighteen inches in length. Each group of six men was escorted by Korean guards and had to produce six cubic metres of wood per day. Therefore, each man had to cut one cubic metre. Each group had to produce a pile of eighteen-inch long logs that was one metre high and six metres in length and stacked beside the railway.

The jungle consisted mainly of teak trees. Being a hard wood, it was notoriously difficult to cut. At first, the Korean guards played fair. The men worked on a 'job and finish' basis for about a month. Then the guards gradually moved the goalposts. As the groups of prisoners got to the end of their six cubic metres, the guards would tell them to cut a half metre more, and then finish. So the men did as they were ordered. Then, having got used to getting six and a half cubic metres, the guards increased it to seven. The prisoners drew the line at this.

They soon worked out ways to lessen their output. They'd start by deliberately felling trees so that they only just missed the guards when they came crashing down. The guards soon stood well away from the working parties. Then, the prisoners would start fetching logs from the piles of previous days. Soon, they appeared to the guards to be producing seven cubic metres of wood in less time than it took to produce the original six. This pleased the guards because they thought that they'd got the extra wood their masters demanded and the work details could still finish early.

It wasn't long until the Railway Regiment checked the actual figures and discovered that about one third of the wood appeared to be missing. The prisoners, of course, were at a loss to explain where it was. The guards had measured and checked each pile; the guards had signed to say that the work was done; so naturally the guards got the inevitable bashing for the shortage!

Soon, these logging operations consumed the trees closest to the railway and the working parties had to penetrate the jungle further to find teak trees. One of the other trees that the prisoners discovered as the work details got deeper into the jungle, was kapok. Kapok is delightfully lightweight and looked just like a teak log to any Korean guard who saw a prisoner 'struggling' with it!

Also, as the Japanese discovered a little later, kapok doesn't burn with enough energy to raise a head of steam for a railway engine. As the prisoners discovered that they could get away with kapok, so the Japanese got more and more of it in their firewood instead of teak. It wasn't long before their trains got stranded at various points on the line, the engines quite literally having run out of steam.

As the logging parties pushed ever deeper into the jungle, the Korean guards tended to be reluctant to follow them too closely, preferring to wait by the portable light railway track that the prisoners used to convey small, hand-pushed wagons of logs to the stacking point. This development was handy for the prisoners. As they got further into the jungle, they started to come across little kampongs of 'bush Chinese'. The people of these little hidden villages were extremely friendly and often gave the starving prisoners food. While four men of each work detail stayed cutting the trees, the other two would slip off to the kampong to trade, but nobody would have stood a chance if they'd been caught. Luckily, no one was.

When Christmas of 1943 arrived, the men at Three Pagodas Pass camp were allowed an extra yasumi day. Bill, Squad Thompson and Danny Pinnock hatched a rather risky plan to provide a good many of their fellow prisoners with a Christmas dinner, the like of which they'd not seen in a long time.

There were about twenty Japanese engineers plus some of the Korean guards in a raised bamboo hut in one corner of the camp, near to the stream. Underneath that hut was a wire enclosure that was home to a group of chickens and some good-sized ducks. The three men decided to try and 'liberate' six of the ducks for Christmas dinner.

Bill and Danny Pinnock had first to train the irrepressible Squad Thompson in the gentle art of silent duck abduction. The trick, apparently, is to grab the duck by its neck. That way, it can't call out. In the meantime, Jimmy Bartlett had almost finished obtaining the necessary ingredients for a large pease pudding, behind the Korean cook's back.

Cooking the stolen ducks wasn't going to be a problem as the prisoners' huts had fires burning in them day and night. Not for heat, but to keep the jungle animals at bay. It was not uncommon for a marauding tiger to surprise everyone at night.

Cometh the hour, the three would-be duck poachers slipped out of their hut at about two in the morning and made their commando-style raid on the duck enclosure. Things appeared to be going well to start with. They'd torn a hole in the flimsy wire of the enclosure and Danny had got his two already. Bill had grabbed one and was just reaching out for his second, when a sudden commotion broke out. Squad Thompson had grabbed a duck by the leg, not the neck! The duck was making such a racket that it seemed as if the whole camp would wake up, especially as the panic-stricken chickens were joining in.

As quick as a flash, the three poachers made for the stream, wringing the ducks necks en route. The guards had all come stumbling out to see what the noise was about. Meanwhile, the three were by the stream, keeping low, while Danny quickly skinned the ducks in the water. As soon as he'd finished, they wrapped the ducks tightly in banana leaves and hurriedly buried them in the ash pit under their hut's fire. They then quickly sneaked back to their beds. The men knew there would be a search pretty soon, so it was best that they were where the guards would expect to find them.

After searching the area around the poultry enclosure and rounding up those chickens that had escaped, the guards did indeed search the huts of the prisoners. Fortunately, they were so enraged and made such a racket as they searched, that they completely failed to notice the faint aroma of slowly roasting duck coming from under their feet!

Finding nothing, the guards left and returned to their angry Japanese masters empty-handed. The prisoners had a smashing Christmas dinner of roast duck, rice and pease pudding the next day and the Japanese had absolutely no idea who had poached their ducks. To the prisoners, the meal seemed to taste even better for that simple fact!

After the Christmas yasumi, the prisoners returned to their logging operations. They were getting deeper and deeper into the jungle by then and were working virtually unsupervised by the guards, who were still not inclined to follow them deep into the forest. This of course led to speculation among the prisoners of a possible escape. It would be so easy to just keep on walking and not return from the logging. The escaping prisoners would have at least three to four hours head start before they would be missed and they were sure that having survived this long, a walk to Mandalay would be like a stroll in the park compared with working on the railway.

But as the proposed escape was examined and discussed, thoughts inevitably turned to those in their ranks who couldn't make the journey; the sick. The men were struck by a vision of what the Japs, furious at their escape, would be likely to do to those that remained, and the men decided they couldn't live with that, so the idea was dropped.

By the end of January 1944, the logging operation at Three Pagodas Pass was finished. The men were told that the camp was to be evacuated and that they would all be sent south to proper Red Cross camps, with better food, better conditions and a long yasumi, which certainly sounded nice. God knows they'd earned it, but something told them that this was just another promise that the Japanese wouldn't live up to. After all, weren't they told the same thing at Singapore?

On one of their last days at Three Pagodas Pass, Jimmy Bartlett suffered a cruel accident. He was cooking rice in a big cauldron sunk into the ground. Stooping to give the rice a good stirring, he slipped and fell into the cauldron. He managed to stay upright, and Bill and Squad got him out and into the cool stream in double-quick time, but he was badly scalded from the waist down. He was sent down the line by train to the hospital at Tamarkan camp for treatment.

About two weeks after Jimmy's accident, the remaining prisoners at Three Pagodas Pass were also evacuated on south-bound trains. They too, ended up at Tamarkan camp.

It was at Tamarkan that the weary, sick, starving, half-dead and abused prisoners were told what their next job for the Emperor was to be.

Chapter Eight

RAIDS, REPAIRS AND RACKETS

The men came down to Tamarkan camp at the beginning of February 1944. There were two camps there, the main and the hospital camps. On arrival, the prisoners were sorted into two groups; those who were going into the main camp and those whose destination was the hospital. Bill was in the latter group, along with Squad Thompson and Washbrook. One of the first things he did was to try and find out what had happened to Jimmy. Unfortunately, Jimmy had been moved out to another camp. Bill never saw him again and still doesn't know to this day whether or not he survived.

Bill was being hospitalized due to several factors. Firstly, his malaria had flared up yet again. Secondly, he had more (though smaller) ulcers on his legs and thirdly, he was also suffering from an acute case of haemorrhoids. An embarrassing ailment at the best of times, there were many of the prisoners who suffered from it because of their poor diet, the bad conditions and dysentery. While Bill underwent treatment, the prisoners in the other group were told what their next tasks were to be.

Some were sent back to Singapore to lengthen the runway at Seletar aerodrome so that Japanese heavy bombers could operate from it. Bill found out later that those poor devils had almost as bad a time of it as they'd had on the railway, having to blast into the hillside and clear a path for the runway extension. Other prisoners were starting to be sent to Japan by ship. Not many of those ever arrived in Japan. The Japanese never marked the ships with a red cross so to an American submarine commander, looking at the convoy through his periscope, it was another collection of Jap supply ships to be attacked. And attacked they were. God alone knows how many prisoners went down with those ships.

Meanwhile, Bill endured a variety of treatments for his ailments. By far the worst was having the course of injections for the haemorrhoids. They were painful to say the least. For ulcers, there were two treatments. Severe ulcers were packed with live maggots and bound in banana leaves for ten days. Less severe cases such as Bill's were allowed a similar, though less repulsive treatment.

The patients used to go and wade in the river up to about waist depth. Then they just stood there while the fish swarmed around their legs and ate away the pus and the bad flesh. It apparently wasn't painful, but it was a peculiar sensation all the same. An added bonus for the patients was the fact that just a little further downstream, those same fish were being caught by the locals and served up as food to the Japanese. Unorthodox though both ulcer treatments may have seemed, nobody doubted their effectiveness.

As Bill began to recover from his ailments he, Squad and Washbrook cottoned-on to another 'racket'. Washbrook had landed himself a job in the Japanese officers' bakery. Although this was often the ultimate insult for a prisoner, having to cook decent, well-balanced meals for the Japanese while existing at starvation point himself, it did have its perks and it wasn't long before Washbrook managed to liberate a sack of tapioca flour. He'd also discovered a way of extracting something like yeast from rotting bananas. Squad and Bill helped Washbrook to liberate fruit and sugar from the bakery too.

Using the stolen flour and Washbrook's yeast, the three men made a sort of bread, baking it in what Bill described as a 'Heath-Robinson' oven that relied on the sun for heat. With the stolen fruit and sugar, the three made what they called 'papaya jam'. They sold the bread and jam at ten cents a slice and it was extremely popular, especially with the hospital patients.

As spring 1944 turned to summer, rumours reached the camp that the Japanese were suffering reverses in Burma. The prisoners heard all sorts of rumours about an Allied offensive there and then one day, Bill thinks it was in June, they saw incontrovertible proof of this offensive. Tamarkan was bombed.

A group of American B-17 bombers, the big four-engined Flying Fortresses appeared over the camp and bombed the railway sidings. On their second run, they came in at low level through the smoke and confusion and strafed the area with machine guns. It was chaos. Everybody – prisoners, Koreans and Japanese – all scattered into the surrounding jungle as the planes swept overhead. Then, they were gone.

The Americans had specifically targeted the rail depot, but some of their bombs had inevitably gone slightly astray. Some of the bombs had landed on the huts of the main camp and about 250 prisoners were killed in that first raid. Bill recalled that it took the Japanese two full days to account for everybody. In the end, there were only two prisoners who were unaccounted for, so they were presumed killed. Bill knew one of them, a man from the 125 Anti Tank Regiment called Tommy Farnborough.

But the truth of the matter was that far from being killed, the two men who were unaccounted for had in fact escaped. It is believed that Farnborough and his companion were the only two British prisoners to have successfully escaped from Thailand.

Apparently, as everyone scattered into the jungle during the raid, Farnborough and his mate had the good fortune to stumble across some men from the Chinese resistance movement. They managed to smuggle the two escapees up-country to the advancing Allied troops whereupon they were put on a flight to India, then home to England.

It wasn't until months later that the surprise news reached Bill by way of a postcard sent to Squad Thompson. The sender of the postcard wrote that they'd been talking to Frankie Starkey recently. Frankie was a friend of Squad's from York whom Bill also knew. It seems that Starkey had bumped into Farnborough, whom he knew, and Farnborough had told him of his escape. Squad couldn't wait to share the news with Bill and anyone else that he could find. This miraculous piece of news boosted morale in the camp for quite a while.

Meanwhile, the American air raids became more and more

frequent. Having fully realized its strategic importance to the Japanese, the Americans had now in fact specifically targeted the Burma-Thailand railway. However, experience had shown that railway lines and bridges were notoriously difficult targets to hit.

But the Americans had a thing called the AZON bomb, the first ever 'smart bomb'. With a 1,000 pound warhead, it was virtually a working prototype for many of today's missiles. What made the AZON 'smart' was the fact that its descent could be controlled. This bomb could be steered. Just as American engineering expertise had been borrowed to construct the railway, it was now American technical expertise that was aimed directly at its destruction.

The AZON had to be dropped from an aircraft at an altitude of between 5,000 and 10,000 feet, but once released, a very powerful flare erupted in its tail. Using the flare as a visual marker, the bomb-aimer in the aircraft used radio-controlled apparatus, not unlike a very large version of that used to fly model aircraft today, to manually steer the AZON bomb directly to its target. Despite one or two teething troubles, the specially trained crews and their AZON bombs were showing a truly remarkable rate of accuracy and unbeknown to practically everyone, it was the smart AZON bomb that had already damaged certain sections of the line and brought down a number of the smaller bridges on the Railway of Death. The AZON bomb remained a closely guarded secret until well after the end of the war.

Most of the prisoners at Tamarkan ended up cursing the American 'fly-boys'. Every time they bombed the railway with that pinpoint accuracy of theirs, it was the prisoners who had to repair the damage they'd done. The Japanese got so angry about it that it was almost like having the 'Speedo' back again.

However, it was due to the repairs necessitated by the American raids that Bill and his cohorts made an important discovery. The local smallholdings bordered the line or the camp in some places. Out repairing the track one day, they discovered that one of the farmers was growing tobacco. Pleading 'benjo' to the guards, the men would hurriedly slip into the tobacco plantation and pick the dead lower leaves from the plants. These leaves were then concealed in the men's loincloths. They now had the means to make cigars!

In between sheltering from American bombers, repairing the Emperor's railway, making cigars, jam-making and baking bread, Bill, Squad and Washbrook found yet another money spinning project to work on – wells. There were many wells around Tamarkan and one thing that the three racketeers had noticed was that the buckets and cans used to draw water from the wells were frequently lost as the frayed ropes often parted under the strain. Eventually, the buckets and cans became a scarcity.

Everyone needed water to drink, so the three used to go down the wells and retrieve the lost cans and buckets. Either Washbrook or Bill would be lowered down the forty-foot shaft on a stout rope. The water was not much more than eight feet deep at the bottom and the lost buckets were almost stacked up. It was comparatively easy to retrieve them, either by diving or simply hooking them with a foot. Once they'd brought them up, they claimed salvage rights. The salvaged containers were then sold back to each hut at ten cents a can. The three had also greatly improved their recipe for burnt-rice coffee by this time, chiefly because they now had limited access to sugar, thanks to Washbrook's job in the bakery.

With the approach of Christmas 1944 Bill, Squad and Washbrook made one or two startling discoveries. The first was that they'd all gained a little weight. The second was that they had amassed the tidy sum of nearly $80 from their nefarious activities, and the third was that by using a little guile, even the normally razor-sharp local traders could be conned.

Some years previously Bill had rescued a sheepdog from the bottom of a well. The RSPCA gave him a medal for it and he'd managed to keep it with him all that time. Needs being most where the devil drives, he used kapok wool to grind off the RSPCA's name and the animal part of the inscription. He then polished it up and managed to convince one of the local traders that it was in fact an Olympic Gold medal for swimming, from the 1936 Berlin games, albeit somewhat worn.

After some tense negotiating, Bill managed to get $40 and four-dozen fresh eggs for it! The eggs were a badly needed source of protein and the $40 bought some other sorely needed food items including a rare jar of Marmite. Naturally, Bill, Squad and Washbrook consumed some of these themselves, but the greater part, as always, went to the hospital.

Bill would like to think that their 'racketeering' helped to save at least some lives as well as their own because every life saved was, as he put it, '. . . one in the eye for the Japs'. Sadly, there's no way he'll ever know to what degree, if any, they succeeded in that for sure.

An unexpected bonus came to the men of Tamarkan camp that Christmas. They actually received a consignment of Red Cross parcels. Mind you, it was one parcel for every twelve men, instead of the one parcel per man that the Red Cross intended. The prisoners were almost grateful to the Japanese for their unexpected 'generosity', until they saw a lot of them walking about smoking Chesterfields or Gold Flakes. Then the prisoners knew that the Japanese had already stolen most of the contents of those parcels.

Though none of them could have known it, the Christmas of 1944 would be the last Christmas they would spend in captivity.

Chapter Nine

THE ROAD TO LIBERATION

No sooner had 1945 arrived than the Japanese sent more prisoners down from Tamarkan camp to fulfil whatever labour requirements they had elsewhere. Bill and his cohorts had been at Tamarkan for a whole year now. The raids by American bombers were almost a daily occurrence and the rumours of the Japanese reverses were becoming increasingly rife and starting to be accurate. Although they'd now come to the conclusion that it was probably just a question of time, they'd come to know the Japanese well enough to doubt that they would surrender as they had. The feeling among the prisoners was that the Japanese would go down fighting to the last man. It was also felt likely that they'd take the prisoners with them.

Another thing that Bill, Squad and Washbrook were sure of was that with so many of the prisoners having been moved out of Tamarkan to work on other projects, it was surely only a question of time before they were deemed fit enough to join them. Although the three men were not glowing with health and vitality exactly, there was no escaping the fact that after a year of their racketeering, they were certainly in better shape than when they'd first arrived.

However, a chance happening kept Bill, Squad and a good many others at Tamarkan for a little while longer. The bridge at Tamarkan was finally seriously damaged in one of the American air raids, though by conventional bombs, not an AZON. Since the bridge was constructed of steel, it required some metal-working skills, as well as a colossal man-effort to get it repaired, so with his blacksmithing skills Bill remained at Tamarkan to work on the bridge.

But eventually, Bill's turn to leave Tamarkan came. About the 10 or 12 June, the Japanese moved a lot of the remaining prisoners out of Tamarkan camp, in two different directions. Bill's senior officer, BSM Ben Pritchett, was among the unlucky ones who were sent on a brutal six-week long, 650-kilometre forced march toward Saigon; a march that claimed the lives of many more prisoners. The ordeal of those on that march ended only with their arrival at a place called Pisnaloke, on 19 August 1945. There, the Japanese guards were arrested and the remaining prisoners freed, five gruelling days after Japan had formally surrendered.

Squad and Bill were among about 2,500 prisoners who were taken up to various parts of Cambodia by lorry. They didn't know it of course, but the Japanese were preparing to make a last stand. For the prisoners bound for Cambodia, it was simply like being on the railway all over again.

They had been brought to Cambodia in order to blast a number of short tunnels into the foothills of the areas that the Japanese were preparing to defend. These tunnels were for the storage of supplies and ammunition that would, in theory, allow the remaining Japanese soldiers to carry on the fight guerrilla-style if they had to.

It really was like old times. First the prisoners had to quickly build their own accommodation and then it was straight into the job in hand, 'Speedo'. The Japanese wanted the job done in double-quick time.

Although the prisoners didn't know it, time was fast running out for the Japanese. By the time the prisoners arrived in Cambodia, it had been nearly six weeks since their German allies had surrendered. The Japanese cabinet had resigned en masse back in April, the Allies had reopened the Burma Road in late January, the Americans were regaining the Pacific theatre and Tokyo had been subjected to numerous air raids by American bombers. The Imperial Japanese Empire was fast crumbling around them.

All the prisoners knew was 'Speedo' though. Bill lost count of the total number of beatings Squad, he and the others got for not working 'Speedo' enough. The trouble was that the Japanese just wanted the job done any old how, but fast. Bill and Squad got into trouble with one particular Japanese engineer because he wanted them to place charges into the roof of the tunnel to make it taller. Bill tried to explain that all it would do was bring the roof down on them, but the engineer wouldn't have it.

In the end, Squad and Bill took a chance and flatly refused to do what he asked. He called the two of them 'bugairo' which was a standard Japanese curse and summoned a couple of the guards, who gave both Bill and Squad 'a right pasting'.

But ultimately, Bill and Squad had the last laugh. As if to demonstrate Japanese superiority, the engineer placed six sticks of gelignite into the tunnel roof himself and detonated it. When the dust finally cleared, he stood in front of what had been the tunnel entrance expecting to be able to admire his handiwork. All he had succeeded in doing was to completely seal the tunnel, exactly the result that Bill had predicted. He cursed the two men loudly again and stormed off. That particular tunnel was abandoned and no more explosives were ever placed into a tunnel roof after that.

Toward the end of July, the prisoners were given another job to do which filled them with a sense of foreboding. The Japanese made them dig a trench right the way around the camp. The trench was six feet deep and the earth from it was made into a sort of embankment on the outside perimeter of the trench. The anxiety of the men was heightened when the Japanese placed heavy machine guns around the top of the embankment. What concerned the prisoners was the fact that the guns were facing *inside* the camp, all the way around. Obviously, it wasn't for defensive purposes. It was pretty obvious to the prisoners that the trench had taken on the look of a mass grave and there was little doubt in their minds as to whom it was for.

But on 8 August, something happened that threw everything into a state of confusion. The prisoners paraded for work as usual that morning but noticed something odd about the behaviour of the Japanese. They were all very jumpy. Eventually, the camp Commandant came out and dismissed them. 'No work today. All men yasumi' he said. The prisoners didn't know what to make of it at all. Unbeknown to them the first atomic bomb had been dropped on the city of Hiroshima two days before and 60,000 people had been killed in an instant.

The uneasy mood continued but the prisoners never did another day's work. On 9 August, the second atomic bomb laid waste the city of Nagasaki. The morning after the second bomb was dropped, the camp resounded to the British 'Reveille' bugle-call. The camp bugler, a man from the Beds and Herts regiment, had gone round to all the huts the night before. It seems he had a local contact on the outside who'd told him 'Japan finished! Big bomb! No fight no more!' Uncertainty ruled, but he decided to take a chance the next morning and use the British wake-up call, not the Japanese one. The prisoners went wild; the Japanese went spare!

But strangely, nobody was beaten or shot. The Japanese still had control by virtue of being armed, but it was obvious to the prisoners that they were now totally subdued. The longed-for hour of deliverance was almost at hand.

Next morning, the prisoners didn't bother to parade for work as the Japanese seemed to be most conspicuous by their absence. There were one or two still around and the camp Commandant was seen once or twice, though he seemed rather preoccupied, but by and large the Japanese and Koreans seemed to have disappeared overnight.

Later that morning, three strangers simply walked into the camp; a British colonel by the name of Knight and two Thai volunteers who wore American uniform. They went straight into the Commandant's office and marched him outside, where they made him hand over his sword in front of all the prisoners. The Commandant was then himself taken prisoner. Any remaining Japanese in the camp either laid down their arms or fled.

The prisoners couldn't believe it! All the worrying they'd done over the imagined suicide tactics of their captors and the vision of them all in that mass grave had thankfully come to nothing. The Japanese had just given up. Colonel Knight then addressed the prisoners, telling them that Japan was expected to formally surrender any day now and that for the men in the camp, the war was over.

Squad and Bill were in the front row during Colonel Knight's speech. Bill still can't describe how he felt that morning. He realized with some embarrassment that there were tears running down his face. He looked at Squad next to him and saw that he wasn't alone in this. A further look round revealed that just about every other prisoner was having exactly the same reaction. There wasn't a dry eye in the house!

I had often noticed during our interviews, that re-living the dreadful memories of his incarceration always had an effect on Bill. Re-living the memory of their liberation had no less an effect on him. It was obvious that the overpowering feeling of relief that he was trying so hard to describe now, was in fact manifesting itself within him all over again. It was one of those moments when his face told the story so much better than his words.

Colonel Knight told the men to remain in the camp, as there were still a number of die-hard Japanese soldiers at large in the area. He also told them that he would arrange for supply planes to make a drop to them the next day.

As Colonel Knight left to make the arrangements for the supply drop, a commotion started in the Japanese cookhouse. Some of the former prisoners had discovered six of the Korean guards hiding in there. The six ex-guards probably thought that being non-Japanese, they'd be all right. Unfortunately for them, this was not the case. What happened next was an act of pure revenge, as the six were savagely beaten up by a growing mob of prisoners before being dragged over to one of the camp's wells. One after the other, the Koreans were thrown down the shaft and the mob then sealed the well with rocks, earth and anything else they could find.

Such behaviour was perhaps understandable after all that the men had endured at the hands of their captors, but Colonel Knight was furious when he found out about it. He told the men that there must be no repeat of those actions. The war was effectively over and whatever the men's feelings on the subject, any repeat of that incident would result in murder charges being brought.

True to Colonel Knight's promise, the next day saw a drop of supplies made to the camp. They'd very thoughtfully sent a radio so that the men could listen to the news. Unfortunately, the men watched with sinking hearts as it came down in a paddy field and was lost before they'd ever had the chance to switch it on. The next few crates to land contained nothing but toothbrushes and toothpaste. All very nice and the men didn't wish to seem ungrateful, but it was food and clothing that they were most in need of.

In the event, any shortcomings in the nature of the supplies didn't really matter to the men anyway. Two days later, a convoy of lorries arrived to transport them all to Bangkok, which was by then securely in Allied hands. On 14 August 1945, Japan formally surrendered. The war really was over.

Chapter 10

REST AND REHABILITATION

As soon as the convoy arrived the men received an issue of new clothing for the first time since 1942. They were all rather too big for them because even the smallest sizes were meant for men in a more normal state of fitness, but it was such a joy for each man to put on a clean T-shirt, clean shorts and a pair of plimsolls. Having discarded their shabby 'Jap-happies' and donned their new clothes, the men were instructed to gather up only personal possessions and in a minimum of time. They didn't mind that at all, as they were only too glad to be leaving the camp. The former prisoners then cheerfully boarded the lorries for a five-hour journey to Bangkok.

By the time they arrived in Bangkok it was late in the afternoon. They were taken to what had been a girls' school and were given accommodation in the old dormitories. As the men settled in, a mobile army decontamination unit was being set up in the playground. As soon as it was ready, the men stripped off and went to have the luxury of a hot shower. It was heaven!

Meanwhile, the clothing that the men had arrived in was collected and burned. When they came out of the showers, they were once again given a fresh issue of clothes. This time they got khaki slacks, a khaki shirt and shoes called 'pumps'; all United States Army issue. They were now deemed to be suitably dressed for dinner.

Dinner consisted of fish and rice after which the men were free to roam about the area in the vicinity of the school. They had to be back by 20:00 hours because there was some entertainment laid on for them.

The first show was a display of kickboxing by some of the local Thai lads and then there was a display of dancing by some of the school's girls. After the display, the men were allowed to dance with the girls but what was strange at first was that this local dancing style didn't involve actual contact with your partner. After a shaky start, they soon got the hang of it.

The next morning, the men boarded the lorries again and were taken to the airport at Bangkok. Upon their arrival, the first thing they saw was a long line of Douglas Dakota aircraft. The convoy came to a halt beside the line of aircraft and the men were assembled on the apron into groups of twenty-five men, one group per aircraft. When they boarded the aircraft, they found that the interior had been completely stripped out and that four wooden benches had been placed lengthwise inside the aircraft's fuselage, two to each side. The men all sat astride these benches which, it was noticed with some apprehension, were not fixed to the aircraft in any way, and the door was slammed shut.

Amid a great roar, the Dakota's twin propellers began to spin as her two Wright Cyclone engines burst into life and the aircraft slowly taxied out to the runway. Suddenly the precariously balanced men all lurched backwards, trying hard to remain on the benches as the aircraft surged forward, gathering speed. The aircraft's tail came up and the Dakota took off and climbed into the sky with the men frantically holding onto anything they could find that seemed remotely solid. Their destination was Rangoon.

Things got more comfortable once the aircraft levelled off and assumed its normal cruising speed. To the men, it seemed rather an unreal world up there. They were flying over Thailand and Burma, the very places from which they'd just been saved. As the aircraft flew on, they could see the tops of mountains sticking up through the clouds. The same mountains they'd blasted a path around for the railway. It all seemed so different looking down on it from the window of the Dakota, knowing that they weren't prisoners any more. No more 'Speedo'. No more beatings. No more starvation and no more deaths. It was unreal.

Soon, the aircraft's engine note changed, as it began its descent and final approach to Rangoon. The landing wasn't quite as hairy as the take-off had been, but the men still had to hang on tightly to something as the wheels bumped down onto the runway. The aircraft taxied over to a group of hangars that had been set aside as a reception and processing area for the returning former prisoners.

The men got off the plane and were immediately taken into one hangar for yet more decontamination treatment. Bill says that they began to appreciate how sheep must feel at dipping time. Once more, their clothing was taken away and burned and the men were issued with a fresh set.

Before they could get into their new clothes, there was a typical army medical inspection to go through. That was when a lot of them got a shock, when they were weighed. Bill weighed six stone, four pounds. That was with the benefit of the weight he'd put on as a result of the 'racketeering' at Tamarkan. Compare that with when he'd first joined the army. In 1939, Bill weighed about twelve and a half stone.

Once through the medical inspection, duly assessed and then dressed in their new clothes, the men were ushered into another hangar. The second hangar was rather more inviting than the first as it was full of tables and chairs that had been set out for dining. There, the men were given a meal of egg and rice and some proper tea to drink, after which they were each given a cablegram form so that they could send a message home. Bill was seated at a table with Squad, Jackie Boyce and Sergeant 'Nabber' Adkins (no relation to the 'Nabber' Atkins mentioned much earlier) and all of them were filling in their cablegram forms when a really pretty young nurse came and stood by their table. She asked if any of them thought they needed a Red Cross nurse. Nabber asked her if she wouldn't mind coming back in about three months and asking him again! The nurse went a bit red, smiled and obviously decided it was time to minister to someone, *anyone*, else!

After processing, the men were taken off to various hospitals in Rangoon, according to their general state of health and any urgent medical needs. Bill can't remember which hospital they ended up in, but he does remember that it was heaven to lie on clean white sheets again, although being in a proper bed rather than one made from bamboo slats took a bit of getting used to. Soon after their arrival, the men were seen by a team of doctors, who would decide upon their course of treatment.

Jackie Boyce, Nabber, Squad and Bill were assessed as being about the same, so they all ended up on the same ward in beds pretty much next to each other. They were put on a five-week course of anti-malarial drugs and each of them was also put on a combination of thirty-three vitamin, iron and protein tablets per day. Food was four small meals a day, which very gradually contained less and less rice and more fresh meat and vegetables. They were also given a lot of milk-based drinks and were told to eat as much fresh fruit as they could. A peculiar thing happened to them after about two weeks of this treatment; they all turned a most unusual shade of bright yellow. At first, they all feared that it was jaundice, but they were told that it was just a side effect of all the vitamin pills they were taking, plus the fact that their bodies were getting used to proper food again. After another week or so, it gradually cleared and they took on a more normal colour.

As Bill and his comrades gradually recovered their health and got more mobile, the confines of the hospital began to tell. For example, Nabber in particular had always had a somewhat colourful turn of phrase, but as restlessness began to set in, he was forever falling foul of the ward's Matron, who was English, about his almost constant swearing. He soon began to look over his shoulder each time before he spoke. Even if he couldn't see her, he'd say something aloud like 'I can't wait to get out of this f***ing place' and, as if by magic, before the last word had left his lips, the Matron would suddenly appear out of thin air right behind him and deliver her customary 'language, Adkins!' in sharp admonishment. Nabber was looking increasingly likely to develop a nervous twitch over it by all accounts!

Even the provision of a somewhat ancient gramophone, initially welcomed by the patients, soon heightened the tensions of confinement. The trouble was that there were only five records, one by Bing Crosby and four by Vera Lynn. After a few days of playing the same tunes in varying order, the most popular request from those patients still confined to their beds was to turn the gramophone off!

Providence lent a hand when the gramophone's wind-up spring finally broke during one playing of Vera Lynn's *The White Cliffs of Dover* and peace once more descended on the ward. But the peace was short-lived. Bill and Nabber took it upon themselves to try to get the gramophone fixed! It was a way of relieving the boredom and also, it would be a great way to sneak out of the hospital when they weren't supposed to!

They had observed that the military personnel who were frequently in and out of the hospital seemed to have a system regarding transport. Jeeps were simply left anywhere. If you 'borrowed' one, it seemed to be perfectly all right so long as the jeep, or another one like it, was returned.

This day, Bill and Nabber waited till the morning rounds were over then without a word, they quickly got dressed, took the gramophone, borrowed a nearby jeep and went in search of an Army Engineers unit. The two men took it in turns to drive and found that it was quite pleasant to be out motoring around in the sunshine. They found a few units by asking various people. At each unit they explained to an engineer that it was for hospital patients, but though the engineers were invariably sympathetic, the consensus of opinion was that the gramophone was beyond repair. Their hopes dashed, the two men decided to head back to the hospital.

They hadn't realized how far their quest had taken them. Not that they were worried, but they had to start asking for directions very soon. The fuel gauge was also noticeably lower by now. It was on this rather circuitous return leg of their journey that they came across another camp, belonging to a South African Rifle Regiment. The two renegade patients decided to give it one last go. Explaining their mission to the sentry on the gate, they were directed to the regiment's workshops. There, they met a South African engineer and explained what they were after. He had a quick look at it and told the two to come back in an hour. Bill and Nabber duly found a 'watering hole' and after a couple of beers, returned to find the gramophone in working order!

The engineer explained to them that he'd managed to weld the broken spring back together. He'd also riveted it for added strength and had carefully filed the whole repair smooth. Although it was now a little shorter than it once was and might not play the whole of a record, it would at least play again. He'd made a superb job of it and Bill thanked him profusely as they left.

The two men eventually returned to the hospital, parking the jeep more or less where they'd found it though without much petrol left in the tank, and returned to their ward to 'face the music' over their little outing. They fully expected to receive a rocket over it, but once the gramophone started to play, the little matter of their unofficial excursion was dropped. Everyone soon ignored even the peculiar 'clonk' that came out of the gramo-phone whenever the repaired section of the spring went round. It just became a part of the overall sound; a sort of mis-timed extra beat.

In mid-September, the patients were all re-evaluated and those deemed now fit enough to travel were told that they were leaving sometime in the next four days. Bill, Squad Thompson, Jackie Boyce and Nabber Adkins were among those classified as being fit enough for the five-week sea voyage home to England.

Chapter Eleven

HOMECOMING

Moored in the docks at Rangoon was a Dutch ship, the MV *Boissevain,* now serving as a hospital transport. She was bound for Liverpool, via the Suez Canal and was destined to be home to Bill, and all the other returning former Japanese prisoners who were sailing on her, for the next five weeks.

The ship left Rangoon on 19 September 1945, or so it says on the medical card that was issued to Bill aboard the ship. They gave the men yet another medical inspection the day after the ship sailed, which was when the cards were issued. They were also given proper British Army uniforms and fresh pay-books too.

In a classic example of understatement Bill's medical card, which he still has, records that he suffered, 'At least thirty attacks of malaria, dysentery and haemorrhoids' during his three and a half years in captivity. It could also have mentioned beriberi, malnutrition, corneal ulcers, skin ulcers, a broken jaw, damaged vertebrae, numerous beatings, crushed stomach muscles, strongoloids, exhaustion and any of a dozen assorted jungle fevers. It is doubtful, however, that there was enough room on anyone's tiny medical card to summarize the suffering they'd all endured during their time as prisoners of the Japanese.

During the voyage home, which included a short spell ashore at Port Said, a series of lectures was given by a regular Army Captain, in order to inform the men of what had happened while they had been isolated as prisoners. They were told how the war had progressed and how, with American help, the earlier 'setbacks' such as Singapore, Burma, the Philippines and North Africa, etc. had all been overcome and the war finally won. They were also told something of how things were at home: Rationing, shortages, destruction of civilian areas by German air raids and rockets. What they weren't told was that most of them had been presumed dead, and that some of them would be in for a shock when they got home.

The voyage itself went well. It was almost like being on a regular liner; good food and plenty of it. The men were even allowed one bottle of beer per man, per day. Good weather too, though they noticed that it got markedly colder as the ship got nearer home. Of course, it was the start of the British winter and after the best part of four years in the tropics, the men had all but forgotten what a British winter was like.

After five more weeks of plentiful, nourishing food aboard the ship, the men were looking fitter than they had been for a very long time. When Bill stepped off the *Boissevain* he was astonished to find that he now weighed just under nine stone. At least, dressed in proper British Army uniform and issued with fresh kit, the men actually looked like soldiers now.

The last shipboard lecture that the men were given by the Army Captain the day before the ship docked, was the one in which they were specifically told that they were not to talk to the press about their experiences. If they did, it would have 'grave consequences' for them and they might even lose their entitlement to a war pension.

He told them all that the war was over now, and that the public didn't want to hear any more about it. He finished his memorable little pep talk by telling the men that:

They especially don't want to be upset by your stories.

Charming! *They*, for whom every one of those men had fought and suffered and died, apparently didn't want to be 'upset' by any stories of what those soldiers had just been through. One can only imagine what must have gone through each man's mind at that point.

On 14 October 1945, the *Boissevain* slowly picked her way

102

through thick fog into the River Mersey and finally docked in Liverpool. Everybody was up on deck, trying to see their first glimpse of England in nearly four years, and they couldn't see anything but the fog! At least it was English fog. The men didn't care about the weather really. Any minute now, they were going to set foot in England again; how good that simple fact must have seemed to them at that point!

As the soldiers disembarked, a band played and it was then that the men realized there were perhaps 1,000 cheering people on the dockside who had turned out to welcome them home. They had made it and were being given a hero's welcome, but they knew only too well that there were many, many more of them who hadn't. It was a sobering thought.

The disembarked troops were quickly organized into groups and put aboard army lorries. Then with their fresh kit slung in after them and civilian girls that had somehow clambered aboard the lorries too, they were driven to a transit camp just outside of Liverpool. Upon arrival at the camp, the girls were ordered out of the lorries and just left by the gate. The funny thing was that none of them seemed to mind that fact one little bit. Or if they did, the troops never heard about it.

The men were kept in camp overnight while leave passes were arranged for them. The next morning, they were all sent on indefinite leave. Bill's next stop was his parent's house in Radway, Warwickshire.

He took the train from Liverpool to Banbury and then a taxi from Banbury station to Radway. He couldn't believe his eyes when the taxi drove up Main Street. It was all decorated in fairy lights and there were banners everywhere, which said 'WELCOME HOME'. Truly, he'd never seen anything like it. As far as the villagers of Radway knew, Bill had been killed in action. The first they knew to the contrary was when Bill's mother received the cablegram he'd sent to her from Rangoon. The original cable that he sent via the Japanese to inform those at home that he was a prisoner, finally arrived a week or so after Bill!

Bill had an emotional reunion with his family but was surprised to find that the girl he'd got engaged to just before the war wasn't there to meet him. His mother explained that believing Bill to be dead, she'd married somebody else about eighteen months previously. At first, Bill wanted to go and see her, to try and sort something out. But after a while thinking about it, he decided not to. No good would have come of it. Bill found out later that there were some poor blokes whose wives, led to believe that they were widows, had later remarried. Compared with that, Bill thought that he had no problems.

The following morning, Bill decided to treat himself. Armed with three and a half year's back pay from the Army, he paid his thirteen-year old brother one shilling for the use of his bicycle. Bill then rode off in search of a suitable pub.

The nearest pub to Radway was at the top of Edge Hill, famous for the battle that was fought there during the English Civil War, but that was up a very steep incline and frankly, Bill didn't fancy the climb. Instead, he elected to cycle the three and a half miles to the neighbouring village of Kineton.

The first pub he came to was called The Carpenter's Arms. Feeling a little saddle-sore by then, it seemed a good enough place for him to stop. Bill was still in uniform because all his old clothes had been given to his brother when Bill was listed as 'missing, presumed killed in action' and his brother had pretty much worn them all out. Entering the pub, Bill walked to the bar and tentatively perched himself on a bar stool. He soon found himself deep in conversation with the only other inhabitant of the pub, Alf Harris, the landlord.

The two men struck up an instant friendship. Alf recognized Bill as the lad from Radway who'd just come home from the Far East. It transpired that Alf had been a Petty Officer in charge of stokers in the Royal Navy during the First World War and was serving aboard the light cruiser HMS *Arethusa* when she was in action against the German Fleet at Dogger Bank in the North Sea in January 1915.

HMS *Arethusa* was the flagship of Commodore Tyrwhitt, commander of the light cruiser and destroyer force that came out from Harwich. During the action she received numerous hits from the German cruisers that were escorting their battleships and she suffered extensive damage. She was thought to be in serious danger of sinking at the time. Alf, like a good many others, was trapped in the engine room of what was widely thought to be a doomed ship. However, *Arethusa* steadfastly remained afloat and managed to limp into Chatham under tow, where the First Lord of the Admiralty, Winston Churchill, met the ship to offer his personal congratulations. But Alf was left with a profound fear of confined spaces as a result of that experience.

Gradually, other customers came in and the pub began to fill, the beer flowed, the dominoes came out and the hours passed by in no time at all. By two in the afternoon, Bill was in no fit state to cycle home. The bicycle stayed at the pub and Bill took a taxi home. For the next four days, Bill commuted by taxi between Radway and The Carpenter's Arms, still paying his brother a shilling a day for the use of his bicycle. At the end of the week, Bill's brother eventually collected the bicycle from the pub on his way home from his carpentry lesson, while Bill continued to enjoy the convivial atmosphere of the bar. Unbeknown to Bill, Alf Harris was instinctively keeping a watchful eye on him.

Over the preceding four days, Bill had been telling Alf a little about the things that he'd been through during his time in captivity, culminating with the fact that his engagement to a local girl had ended while he was away and that he had only just discovered the fact. Alf told Bill that by a strange coincidence, his daughter, Beryl, had just had a broken romance and would be coming home for the weekend from her job as a dental nurse in a Birmingham practice. Noticing that Bill had been putting away quite a few pints of beer over the past four days, possibly to blot out some hurt, Alf told Bill that in his opinion, his daughter would be just the sort of girl to calm Bill down. Without Bill realizing it, Alf had planted a seed and was now quietly standing back to watch it grow.

As Alf had also suffered badly from shell shock as a result of his experiences and now knew at first-hand the signs of what is today called 'post-traumatic stress disorder', he'd been watching

Bill, and perhaps saw something of that in him. Also, by all accounts, Alf could never resist a spot of matchmaking and he perhaps saw it as a way of solving two problems at one stroke! On the brighter side of course, one didn't tend to argue with Alf because he'd also twice been the runner-up for the title of Lightweight Boxing Champion of the Royal Navy.

That Saturday morning, the matchmaking Alf formally introduced Bill to his daughter, Beryl. Bill was invited to stay to lunch after which he took her to a local football match. They soon discovered that they had quite a lot in common. After their afternoon outing, the couple returned to the pub, where Bill also stayed to tea, before he finally took a taxi home that evening. He was back again the following day, for Sunday lunch. Bill decided that he rather liked Beryl, so after that weekend, to save himself money on taxi fares, he went out and bought a car.

About two weeks after he came home, the villagers of Radway decided to hold a 'Welcome Home' dance in Bill's honour, at the village hall. During the proceedings, Bill was presented with a cheque for £450, which represented the amount raised by the collection that had secretly been taken round the village. He was delighted at first, but at about half past ten in the evening, a group of Italian prisoners entered the hall and started dancing with the local girls. Bill was told that this had been allowed at previous functions and that the prisoners were waiting to be repatriated. Bill however, was not at all happy about this state of affairs and told the Italians in no uncertain terms that they were to leave, immediately.

The sudden departure of the Italians caused an awkward pause in the evening. Bill was angry that those former enemy soldiers should have been invited to his dance, and he thinks it showed. He just stood there in the middle of the hall, looking all around him, and then remembered the cheque that was in his pocket. He took it out, tore it up into little pieces and threw the bits into the air saying the whole village could 'stuff it' if they thought he would like a party with former enemy soldiers as a homecoming. Then he left.

Two days later, two members of the village committee came

to see Bill, to ask him to reconsider and to accept a replacement cheque. Bill refused on principle, but he told them that if they wanted to give the cheque to his mother, who had thought her son dead for three and a half years, that would be all right. That is exactly what the village committee did.

Chapter Twelve

SETTLING DOWN

About four weeks after Bill got home, Beryl was kicked rather sharply under the kneecap by a patient who was under anaesthetic. As Beryl had contracted poliomyelitis at the age of just three months and had undergone various treatments and operations since, this sort of mishap did her no good at all. Bill and Beryl decided that she would not go back to work. Instead, she and Bill got engaged that November and she spent every day with her future husband.

Alf Harris prompted the couple toward marriage with the offer of the flat above the pub. Bill and Beryl decided to get married on the last day of 1945. It was a good way to leave the past behind them and set out on a new life and the New Year together.

The wedding took place at St Peter's church, Kineton, at 11:30 a.m. It was scheduled for 11:00, but as Bill stood waiting at the church with Squad Thompson acting as his best man, it became apparent that the bride was going to be more than a little late. Frankly, by 11:20, Bill was beginning to wonder if she would show up at all!

Unbeknown to Bill, Alf had inadvertently locked everyone, including himself, out of the upstairs section of his pub. By the time he'd taken a fire axe to the door and retrieved the situation, it was almost 11:20. The bride hadn't finished dressing either. She finally arrived at the church at 11:28 wearing a beautiful white dress, a white veil and black bedroom slippers! That seemed to set the tone for the rest of the day.

The wedding ceremony finally went ahead without a hitch and

the reception was just fine. After that, Squad, Bill and about fifteen other ex-POWs went back to Alf's pub and put paid to the remaining sixteen gallons of ale that Alf had in stock while Beryl changed.

Somewhat the worse for drink Bill then decided to drive his new bride to their planned wedding night at the Swan Hotel, in Stratford-upon-Avon. Things appeared to be going splendidly till Bill hit a set of railings at Challcote Park. Neither of them was hurt and the car wasn't badly damaged, but Bill had managed to strip the park's railings off for about twenty-five feet. As Bill and Beryl quickly departed the scene, the park's deer began to escape through the new gap in the railings.

Upon arrival at the Swan Hotel, the couple were refused entry. They couldn't prove that they were married. In those days, the marriage certificate wasn't issued straight away. The newlyweds had to wait a couple of days and then go and collect it from the church. Without the certificate, the hotel receptionist refused to let them in.

Determined not to let things spoil their day, the couple went in search of alternative accommodation. They found a restaurant called 'The Sugar Loaf' that also provided bed and breakfast facilities and wasn't as stuffy about the marriage certificate as the hotel. The couple booked in then sat down to a roast meal. They were having a marvellous time till a still slightly intoxicated Bill accidentally shot a roast potato across the restaurant!

Thinking that he had committed the ultimate breach in restaurant protocol, Bill stood up and apologized, explaining that they were just married and that it was a case of wedding night nerves. With that, everybody in the restaurant started congratulating them and buying them drinks. They had a high old time of it! The next morning, as the couple came down to breakfast, all the other guests and the staff were giving them 'that knowing look' and smiling at them. It was a little embarrassing, but Bill and Beryl didn't really mind. To be honest, they found it rather fun!

Later that morning, Bill and Beryl returned to Kineton, stopping off en route to pick up Squad Thompson and his wife, Frankie. Then, after collecting their marriage certificate, it was off to York. They had an overnight stop at Leicester at the Bell Hotel, but as they'd arrived late, they'd missed dinner. Squad and Bill left the girls at the hotel and went off to get fish and chips for them all. When they got back, the two men found that the girls had been keeping themselves occupied during their absence with a large sherry bottle. To say that the girls were somewhat intoxicated was putting it mildly!

The four set off again the next morning but only got as far as Doncaster, as one or two certain members of the party were not really up to the journey the next day! The four of them finally got to York the day afterwards, late again, and just in time to find that their rooms had been let out to some other people. They managed to find another hotel soon enough and the four friends spent the remaining days of Bill and Beryl's honeymoon together, having a marvellous time as only four such close friends could. But lurking under all the gaiety was the beginning of the nightmare that was to haunt Bill for the rest of his life, triggered by a sudden recurrence of malaria.

Bill woke up one night in January 1946 in the grip of a malaria attack. Having suffered them many times as a prisoner, he knew exactly what it was. He thought it was no big deal and that he could cope with it. He wasn't prepared for the vivid nightmares that followed, though.

Beryl says that it has been the same for years. He spends ages violently thrashing about in bed, then the real kicking and screaming starts. She tries to calm him, but can't wake him from it. Suddenly, Bill is apt to fly out of bed and that is usually when he wakes up.

Asked if he can recall what it is he dreams about, Bill is still unsure exactly how the nightmares start, but he always seems to end up running. On the march back to camp in the evening, the Japanese guards used to get jumpy if the working parties of the day shift were out in the dark, so they used to tell them to hurry up. Those at the back of the column were beaten till they overtook their comrades, who of course would be next in line for a beating as soon as they became the back markers. Therefore, nobody wanted to be at the rear of the column, so the prisoners all ended up running, trying to overtake as many men as they could so that someone else got the beating. That is what Bill calls 'the running nightmare', but it is far from the only one he has.

Other nightmares involve reliving the things he suffered at the hands of the Japanese and Koreans. Things like digging his own grave, the 'sporting torture' or being savagely beaten for no particular reason other than a guard's impatience. Sometimes, the nightmares revolve around what *might* have happened to him had the Japanese or Koreans gone a stage further in their abuse of him. Sometimes, the nightmares are of the things Bill has seen done to other prisoners, being done to him instead.

Whatever the subject of the nightmares, they are all horribly real to Bill at the time and are almost always accompanied by some form of bizarre behaviour. This can range from filling his slippers with urine, a semi-comical leftover trait that stems from their not being allowed out of the hut after dark, even to answer a call of nature, to acts of extreme violence. He has smashed many of Beryl's ornaments during his nightmares. Even now, nearly sixty years on, he has destroyed bedside cabinets in his sleep. Beryl doesn't know where he gets the strength. She's seen him lift and hurl items of furniture in his sleep that he wouldn't ordinarily attempt to move while he's awake! She says that it's quite frightening, really.

After the first few occurrences, Bill thought that maybe he needed to go back to work, to take his mind off it. In April of 1946, Bill duly found himself a job and Beryl discovered that she was pregnant. The baby was born in October of that year, with a profound heart defect. It was a boy, whom they named Alfred, after Beryl's father. Sadly, Alfred lived only six days. A study carried out much later revealed that an astonishing eighty per cent of former Far East POWs lost their first-born child afterwards. The predominant cause seemed to be heart defects. Bill attributes this to the malnutrition they suffered as prisoners and the concentrated cocktail of drugs and vitamins that they were given in hospital just after they were liberated.

Bill was working as a builder and even at work, the pent-up anger and frustration that he carried within would sometimes come out, usually with spectacular results. He'd always said after he came home, that nobody would ever tell him what to

111

do, ever again. Ask, and the chances are that he would do it. Order him, and there'd be trouble!

On one job, in the space of a single morning, Bill laid out the site foreman, the clerk of the works and the sub-agent. It was all over bonuses. The aforementioned three were on a fiddle at the workers' expense. Bill proved it and directly confronted them with it, but they just gave him that 'so what are you going to do about it?' look; it was sheer contempt that they displayed. He'd seen that contemptuous expression so many times before on Japanese faces and been totally unable to do anything about it. This time, he *did* do something about it. Needless to say, Bill did not keep his job at that particular site.

Bill then had a succession of jobs rebuilding bomb-damaged Britain. His favourite was churches. That was exactly the kind of quality work that Bill really enjoyed. It called for all his skills not only as a builder, but also as a stonemason. The repair had to be invisible, especially around stained-glass windows. Sometimes, he'd be cutting a damaged stone that was 500 years old, completely in half. Then he'd have to replicate the good half in modern stone, put the modern half on the inside of the repair where it wouldn't be seen and the original half on the viewed side with an invisible join between the two. He would also have to blend the mortar so as to be indistinguishable from the original in appearance. Bill also worked on repairing a brewery, as well as several RAF stations.

In 1948, their son Jeremy was born. Three years later, their second son, Terry, arrived. In 1958, Bill and Beryl decided to take up the British government's offer of an 'assisted passage' to emigrate to Australia. They just needed a little more money before embarking on the trip that would change their lives, hopefully for the better.

Bill took a job with a building contractor called Dolphin Developments. His job involved travelling to different parts of the country. One project was the building of a village called Allhallows-on-Sea, on the Kent side of the Thames estuary, opposite Southend. It was while Bill was working here, that Beryl suffered a relapse of her poliomyelitis. At the same time, Bill suffered a complete mental breakdown.

It wasn't anything dramatic to start with. Bill had finished work for the day and was driving home. A few hours later, he pulled up in the village of Radway in Warwickshire. Of course, he should have been in Allhallows in Kent. The trouble was, although the people in Radway knew who he was, Bill, himself, didn't anymore. It was as if the involuntary drive up there had washed everything away.

Total amnesia had set in and Bill was admitted to Ward 2 in Roehampton Hospital, which was solely for the treatment of former Far East prisoners. He stayed there for the next six months, until his memory gradually returned. During his absence, Beryl too had been hospitalized. The family was further divided as one son was cared for by each set of grandparents. It was a dreadful time. Beryl had never dreamed that her polio could come back and as for what suddenly happened to Bill, it was almost too much for her to bear.

When Bill was finally released from the hospital the family were reunited once more, but the trip to Australia was now clearly out of the question. Beryl's relapse had left her partially paralysed. With Beryl now unable to travel, they decided to stay in Allhallows.

It was just afterwards that Bill discovered the FEPOW (Far East Prisoners of War) Association. He says that they were marvellous towards Beryl and him. Unknown to Bill, FEPOW had stepped in on his behalf while he was in Roehampton and their welfare fund had assisted Beryl financially till he was back on his feet. Both Bill and Beryl soon became active members. There was the Japanese Labour Camps Survivors Organisation too.

In 1961, Bill and a former workmate started their own building company called Trojanwood Limited. They started out by sub-contracting. The business soon flourished and they gained several important contracts in the south and south-east of England. After nine prosperous years, Trojanwood Ltd. found itself under increasing competition from less professional builders, or as Bill still prefers to call them, 'Cowboys', and the decision was reluctantly taken to fold the company.

Bill then went back 'on the cards' as a stonemason and found employment with a company called Gravesend Stonemasons. The time he spent working for them was the happiest ten years of his working life. Gravesend Stonemasons had a rolling contract with the National Trust and Bill was permanently posted to the beautiful Knole House in Sevenoaks, Kent; a lovely stately home with a huge park full of deer. That really was top quality work. Bill found that everybody who worked there was a craftsman and more to the point, each was readily acknowledged as such.

As if to prove the point, Bill has a hand-made wooden fruit bowl that a friend made for him as a present, out of the pruned branches of many of the park's great trees. You cannot help but admire it for the sheer workmanship that so obviously went into making it. Bill says that you won't find anything like that anywhere nowadays. He was quite correct about the bowl. Furthermore, he could just as easily be talking about himself, if only he realized it.

Chapter Thirteen

COMING TO TERMS

At the age of sixty-three, Bill opted for early retirement. Two years later, he and Beryl decided to purchase their council bungalow under the tenants' discount scheme that was introduced at that time. Previously, the couple couldn't even qualify for life insurance, mainly because of Bill's wartime injuries, but this scheme was just the thing for them. It is often said that the Devil makes work for idle hands. As soon as the sale was agreed, the retired builder and stonemason started making all the alterations to the bungalow that his professional brain had been cataloguing for the past fifteen or more years. The result is a tailor-made home that suits their every need perfectly.

In 1985 it was the fortieth anniversary of the end of the war. As Bill and Beryl were active members of both the FEPOW Association and the Japanese Labour Camps Survivors Association, they attended many functions and events. It was during the course of one such event that Bill told a newspaper the story of how he'd 'doctored' his RSPCA medal and traded it for much needed food. The newspaper informed the RSPCA of the story and the RSPCA duly presented Bill with a replacement medal, free of charge.

1995 saw both the fiftieth anniversary of the end of the war and Bill and Beryl's golden wedding anniversary that December. The couple decided to have it a little early, in the summer, as December was a bit too cold for them by now. The party was duly held that August. Beryl and Bill say that it was a lovely day. About ten of his old Army pals were able to attend including Ben Pritchett, Cyril Hullcup and Dickey Francis. Sadly, one face that

115

was missing from the gathering was Squad Thompson. Squad had died sometime previously. His marriage to Frankie broke down and although he later remarried, he moved away and Bill and Beryl still don't know where he went. They heard later on the ex-POW grapevine that he'd passed away.

The following year, 1996, saw an old ghost come back to haunt Bill and a lot of his fellow ex-prisoners. On Thursday, 15 August Bill, like a good many others, was quietly reading his copy of the *Daily Mail* newspaper when a frighteningly familiar face leapt off the page. Bill literally jumped when he saw it, but worse was to come. By the time he had finished reading the full-page article, he was in a frenzy of hatred. Without warning, Bill jumped up, completely cleared a shelf of Beryl's porcelain ornaments and promptly punched a hole clean through the bathroom door. The full force of the nightmare had returned, larger than life and twice as ugly. Many more sleepless nights lay ahead.

The subject of that newspaper article was a ceremony that the Japanese were apparently holding in Tokyo to mark the fifty-first anniversary of the end of the war. In Tokyo stands an old railway locomotive, bearing the head-plate number C5631. It is a dedicated shrine to the men of the Imperial Japanese Army's Railway Regiments. Engine No. C5631 was used on the Burma-Thailand railway from 1943 onwards and the Japanese had 'brought it home' sometime previously.

A large part of the *Daily Mail's* article was an interview with a Japanese man who was a former officer of the Imperial Japanese Army's 9 Railway Regiment. A renowned train enthusiast and now the proprietor of a Tokyo camera shop, this man told the newspaper that the British prisoners had only hated the Japanese because they had made them work. He further stated that the prisoners were just lazy men who'd wanted nothing more than an easy life. Asked by the reporter about the atrocities, he claimed, 'Human rights were not a priority then'. He further stated that he personally did not feel any remorse, that the Japanese had done nothing to be ashamed of and that the prisoners had at least died in a good cause as the railway, of which he was intensely proud, was still operating today. Bill recognized the man's face in the newspaper photograph from the camp at Tarsao. It was that of Sugano.

The pictures accompanying the article are of a young Sugano posing on the front of Engine C5631 on the Burma-Thailand railway in 1943; Sugano at the Tokyo engine shrine fifty-three years later and a rare photo showing the weakened men of Bill's camp struggling to carry a sack of rice between four of them. Pressed by the newspaper for a response, the Japanese Embassy in London refused to condemn Mr Sugano's remarks, sparking further outrage.

Bill was one of many who wrote indignant letters to the press that day. The chairman of the Japanese Labour Camps Survivors Association, Bill Holtham, himself a survivor of the railway, said that he would very much like to meet Mr Sugano face to face though not to warmly shake his hand in the spirit of conciliation between former enemies. No, what Bill Holtham said he had in mind was shaking Mr Sugano warmly by the throat on behalf of all ex-prisoners. Both Bill Reed and Bill Holtham, like so many others, wanted to know how anybody, especially someone like Sugano of all people, could say such things. As both men and indeed every other surviving ex-prisoner would like to remind you, the Japanese in charge of that railway literally got away with wholesale murder.

It should be noted that Mr Sugano was never specifically charged with any war crime through lack of any hard documentary evidence directly linking him to the appalling abuse of prisoners. Mr Sugano has subsequently stated that: 'The construction (of the railway) was undertaken in wartime, an unusual time.' Whilst he now 'sincerely regrets their (the POW's) deaths' he also thinks 'that is the reality of war'.

At another of the camps on the Burma-Thailand railway, Songkurai, the Japanese Chief Engineer was, like Mr Sugano, also an officer of the 9 Railway Regiment. His men liberally used wire whips to spur the prisoners in his charge to greater efforts (or premature death) during their construction of the Emperor's railway. Bill Holtham, by a miracle, was a survivor of Songkurai.

Given such triggers, how does one live with an ex-prisoner like Bill Reed? Beryl, (who ought to know) says that it can be very difficult at times, but she thinks that Bill is worth it. The problem is that Bill simply will not give in to anything, particularly his own sufferings. She says that she can hardly blame him for that, with what he's been through during the time he was a prisoner. Giving in then would have meant his certain death. Those experiences changed Bill forever, but he can't just wipe it out now, because the human mind isn't like that.

Although time has helped a little towards the healing of his mental scars, Bill still has a physical legacy of the time he spent as a prisoner of the Japanese. He still has skin ulcers that simply will not heal and he has got used to dressing them himself. Malaria has substantially weakened his heart, as have the strongoloids that went untreated for so long. Thanks to the 'sporting torture' of the guards, most of Bill's lower digestive tract now resides in an incurable football-sized hernia that has been created by the destruction of a number of his stomach muscles. The vertebrae that were fractured by Japanese rifle butts also cause him pain and prevent him from standing to his full height.

So to what does Bill attribute his survival? How did he over-come the despair, the misery and the sheer frustration, as well as the mental and physical abuse? He says that first and foremost, one had to adapt to the surroundings, no matter how bad things got. The prisoners soon got used to eating things like snakes, lizards and even small monkeys when they could catch them. One of the best meals Bill remembers as a prisoner was when he had his first taste of cooked python.

But there were a lot of men who just couldn't bring themselves to eat such things and those men died, because the human body simply cannot survive on foul rice and the odd chunk of dried fish for very long at all. Add the regime of unbelievably hard labour and disease to the equation, and one doesn't have to be a genius to realize that one's days were numbered.

Also, Bill says that you had to have good mates around you. Loners soon lost it and died. Some men were afraid to take chances like stealing food from the Japanese. Once he'd had a few beatings for it, Bill soon realized that the worst the Japanese could do to him was to kill him. Without the food, he'd have died anyway, so what was there to lose? He supposes that it came down to a team spirit or comradeship, but they all tried to look out for each other as much as possible. The key to the whole thing was putting yourself last, not first, and not to waste a thing.

Also, if you were put to work in the kitchens preparing food for the Japanese, opportunities frequently arose to gain the odd pyrrhic victory. It was by no means uncommon for a prisoner to add to the food some especially disgusting ingredient of his own behind the Korean cook's back. Spit was easy, but urine was always a 'hot favourite' though even that was by no means the most disgusting ingredient that a prisoner ever added to their captors' meals.

Did the prisoners ever try to sabotage the railway? Frequently! Quite apart from the early example that we've already seen of the specialist prisoners in the surveying parties shifting the marker pegs, prisoners working on bridge building often buried swarms of white ants or termites under the wooden piles, fervently hoping that the ants would eat away the pile and cause the structure to collapse, preferably while a train full of Japanese troops was crossing overhead! Opportunities for real, direct structural sabotage were rare, though if they cropped up, they were taken and certainly some rotten wood found its way into various parts of the railway's infrastructure, but generally the Japanese engineers scrutinized everything very closely indeed.

Mostly, the prisoners resorted to delaying tactics, especially at tenko, during which the men would be given the shouted command to 'bango'. The prisoners then had to number off, in Japanese of course, which always provided an opportunity for deliberate counting errors. Eventually, the Japanese grew tired of the constantly differing number of assembled prisoners and ended up counting the prisoners three times just to be certain of the actual number going to work that day. It was amusing for the prisoners to watch as an apparently innumerate guard got a slap from the supervising officer for his presumed inability to count and it used up precious construction time too.

Other delaying tactics were used by the prisoners in their attempts to slow the pace of the railway's construction and, of course, one mustn't forget that locomotives simply couldn't run on kapok wood!

However, there is a marked tendency these days to think that events such as those that are described in this book are best forgotten. One will often hear comments such as: 'It was such a long time ago; what's the point in keeping it alive?' or, '. . . it is hardly relevant to today', '. . . it is best left in the past', '. . . time to move on' or even that '. . . it doesn't matter now'. Some even say that such old wounds are best left to heal quietly. Quite apart from the fact that these wounds, both the physical and the mental ones, *never* heal, no matter how much time elapses, there is a very real danger in forgetting what happened, however long ago it may have been. It doesn't pay to become complacent toward the teachings of history.

The exact number of people who actually died building the Burma-Thailand railway is not known. What is known is that at least 15,000 British, Dutch, Australian and American prisoners were mercilessly sacrificed to its construction. What is often not realized is that between 80–85,000 Asian civilian labourers, in a lot of cases entire families with children were also sacrificed to the building of the Emperor's railway. Their deaths went completely unrecorded and their bodies lie in mass graves, deep in the Thai jungle.

Just as Hitler sought to exterminate the Jewish race and any others that failed to meet the Aryan standard, so the Japanese sought to exterminate the more 'inferior' Asiatic races. It will be recalled that Bill witnessed such acts as early as the fall of Singapore. South-east Asia had its very own 'holocaust' too it would seem, albeit not on such a grand scale as the Germans organized for their attempted extermination of the Jews.

Does Bill still hate the Japanese as a race? 'No', he says. 'Well, not anymore.' He used to, at first, but one can't keep hating and he feels that those Japanese who were not born then, or who were too young to have been a part of it, do not deserve such treatment anyway. No, it is very much the wartime Japanese that Bill hates and frankly always will. Such arrogantly insensitive residual types like the Suganos of this world certainly don't help to change that.

Bill still maintains that if the Japanese had fed them properly, looked after them with proper medical supplies and not sadistically abused them, then the prisoners would probably have built that railway willingly. But they were treated as something worse than slaves. They were not human beings in the eyes of their captors and the Japanese have never apologized for that, not sincerely.

Of the Japanese who have prominently figured in Bill's story, the former commandant of Tonchan camp, Tiger Hiramatsu, was hanged as a war criminal in 1946. Strangely perhaps, Bill feels that his fate was undeserved. Bill says that Tiger could be 'a most unreasonable bastard' when he wanted to be, but he was under intense pressure from his superiors to meet his quotas. Bill always felt that Hiramatsu tried to be fair and that he was an honourable man; a career soldier who was eventually torn between what he believed to be right and what his superiors demanded of him. He knew full well the price of failure in the Imperial Japanese Army. Personally, Bill says that he wouldn't have wanted to be in Tiger's shoes for the world.

General Tomoyuki Yamashita, the man who took General Percival's surrender at Singapore, was also executed after the war. If Tiger Hiramatsu's fate was seemingly unjustified, then that of General Yamashita would appear to be doubly so.

Yamashita was without doubt a very honourable man who rigidly followed the Japanese Samurai code and traditions. He once described the fall of Singapore as the greatest military bluff he'd ever known. At the time he met General Percival at the Ford Motor factory, Yamashita's troops were already suffering marked shortages of general supplies, ammunition and above all, water. Yamashita was impatient for Percival to sign the formal surrender, before his own desperate situation became known. 'If I had been made to fight any longer for Singapore, I would have lost completely. Just six more days of fighting would have ensured my complete defeat,' he said.

Captured on 2 September 1945, Yamashita was tried in Manila by the Americans, who found him guilty of atrocities on the extraordinary pretext that he was in overall command of the troops who systematically sought to eradicate Singapore's civilian Chinese population. This verdict was reached even though the Americans couldn't produce a shred of evidence to show that Yamashita had ever ordered, condoned or even knew of such an operation.

Yamashita, it would seem, was simply 'guilty by association', by virtue of his being the higher authority of those individuals who actually committed the crimes, even if Yamashita himself was unaware or ignorant of them. He was hanged as a war criminal on 23 February 1946. Rough justice indeed, especially when one considers that nearly sixty years on, there are still certain Japanese individuals who, if judged by the same standards as Yamashita was, should have suffered the same fate as he did. Yet because they were not so high ranking and also could not perhaps be directly linked to the appalling abuses of their fellow human beings, they are allowed to remain at liberty today, despite their indelibly bloodstained hands, in what is often termed 'the spirit of forgiveness'. Failing that, they can, of course, always hide behind the niceties of today's bizarre legal constraints. But they do at least know who they are, and what they have done. Suffice to say that it is fervently hoped by a good many, that all such persons ultimately find that their consciences do not permit them to rest, ever.

But if some of the guilty cannot receive their due recognition, then we can at least go some way towards balancing that by a further mention of one of the truly good. Everyone's favourite guard, Big Joe, finished the war at the officers' camp at Kanchanaburi. It was at Kanchanaburi that Big Joe had saved the life of Colonel Toosey's interpreter, Captain Drower. A sadistic Japanese officer, Captain Naguchi, once had Drower kicked and beaten to the point of insensibility and then buried alive in a large hole covered with heavy bamboo matting and with only a bamboo pipe providing air for Drower to breathe. Big Joe used to sneak out to the place during rest periods and at night, secretly passing food and water to Drower down the pipe.

When news of the Japanese surrender reached Kanchanaburi, Big Joe stopped a British lieutenant who was digging a latrine trench. Joe told the lieutenant that Japan was finished. He then took over the digging of the latrine himself.

As the years go by, the number of people with first hand memories of those days grows ever smaller. Even the railway itself shrinks and what is left of the Burma-Thailand railway no longer connects those two countries, as the jungle slowly but resolutely reclaims what was taken. A modern-day intrepid explorer following the original line of the railway will find that Hellfire Pass is now preserved as a monument to those who died cutting it, but much of the line north of there is now largely overgrown and the track is buried beneath a dense carpet of jungle foliage. If he is persistent enough to press on further up the line, our explorer will be rewarded when he suddenly finds an abandoned locomotive sitting in the middle of the jungle; probably stranded after trying to run on kapok wood.

At Tamarkan, large numbers of tourists, (including, incidentally, Mr Sugano, who is a regular visitor) still visit the bridge, paying good money to cross it very slowly on a diesel train or on foot. The bridge itself was finally brought down in June of 1945. About a week after Bill left Tamarkan camp to go to Cambodia, four American B-24 Liberators came in at treetop height and each aircraft deposited a very well aimed 1,000-pound conventional bomb at the foot of the central bridge pier. The central pier collapsed and two of the spans came down with it. By the time the line was re-opened, Japan had surrendered.

Only about a quarter of the original railway is still in use today and sixty years on, Bill and his kind certainly need no reminding of what happened there. But they won't be around forever. In the end, all that will remain will be a few old books, a historically inaccurate movie and part of a railway in a remote region of Thailand that was literally paid for with blood. That is why we must never forget what those men went through.

Bill wanted to call this book *Lost Souls of the River Kwai* (despite the inaccuracy of the river's title!) because so many of his friends are buried in unmarked graves in the Thai jungle, or in mass graves where the camps used to be. At least one quarter of Bill's regiment, the 85 Anti-Tank, died as prisoners of the Japanese. But Bill also wanted it to be remembered that those who survived and came home, still left a great part of their soul in the Thai jungle too: a separation that can never be wholly rectified until the survivors finally rejoin their fallen comrades. It is at Bill's request therefore, that his story ends with a small piece of poetry. It is these few lines, written by Laurence Binyon and familiar to many, which Bill uses to remind himself daily of the lost souls.

They shall not grow old as we that are left grow old.
Age shall not weary them, nor the years condemn.
At the going down of the sun, and in the morning,
We will remember them.

AUTHOR'S POSTSCRIPT

In March 2003, I was privileged to meet Bill's former Battery Sergeant Major, Ben Pritchett. Ben, it will be recalled, was their senior man once the Japanese had removed all the British officers at the start of the terrible 'Speedo' period. Even today, Ben is still looked upon as a father figure by those men who survived and were under his command. For my part, I found myself faced with a sprightly nonagenarian; an irrepressible character who also had his own collection of anecdotes, (though he freely admitted that perhaps not all of them were altogether true!)

In May 1981, Ben and a party made up of 101 fellow ex-prisoners and their wives, returned to the Thai jungle with the Oldham branch of the FEPOW Association. The party was there to visit the war cemeteries, the bridge and many of the sites of the former labour camps where they were incarcerated.

They travelled by air, by river and finally by train on the very railway they had built. At one point on the rail journey near Wampo, Ben exclaimed aloud that he didn't know who had laid that particular section of the track that they were travelling on, but it was awfully bumpy! Thus did he display that very British sense of humour that had undoubtedly contributed to their survival.

Ben also told me, with his typically ex-Sergeant Major's humour, that he remembered the time when Bill and Sergeant Cyril Hullcup came to Tonchan South camp with the Japanese engineers, in preparation for the blasting work on Hellfire Pass.

I asked the two of them what the bloody hell they thought they were doing with the Jap engineers. Bill told me that they'd been attached to them as explosives specialists. Well, once I'd finished laughing, I told the pair of them that the Japs must be desperate, because I personally wouldn't have trusted either of them to safely blow their respective noses, let alone a limestone cutting for a bloody railway! The fact that they managed to do it without killing themselves or anybody else around them is a source of constant amazement to me!

I asked if the fate of Lieutenant Carpenter, who'd refused to leave his men when Singapore fell, was known. 'I saw him once or twice in the camps,' said Ben, 'but once the Japs took all the officers away I didn't see him anymore.'

'I know he made it,' said Bill, 'because he went to start a new life in South Africa after the war.' Sadly, it seems that the nightmare also caught up with Carpenter. He apparently died some years afterwards in a South African mental asylum, having suffered a total breakdown. Tragically, it is the all too common fate of these men.

I also had the pleasure of meeting Colonel Tim May, also formerly of the Queen's Own Oxfordshire Yeomanry, who very kindly agreed to write the foreword to this book, and June Osbourne, wife of the late Jack Osbourne who was a lieutenant serving in Bill's regiment at the time they were taken prisoner.

After a successful career in banking, during which time Jack Osbourne also stood as the then youngest Conservative candidate for Hammersmith South, Jack found time to give talks about his wartime experiences. Jack, it seems, never forgot the day that Big Joe saved Captain Drower's life at Kanchanaburi, at such obvious and inordinate risk to himself. Nor did he forget Big Joe stopping him from digging that latrine trench to tell him that the war was over, then taking over Jack's work. Jack never failed to mention Big Joe in any of the talks that he gave.

Another point that emerged from Jack Osbourne's lecture notes was that the British chain of command in Singapore was lamentable. Officers in the field were given no briefings, no idea of even the local, let alone the general, situation and above all, absolutely no clear instructions or objectives. In his notes, Jack recalled that he was once ordered to rendezvous with an unknown brigadier at a position that the Japanese had in fact overrun some three days before! It was on his way to that supposed rendezvous that Jack met quite a lot of Australian troops coming the other way, retreating. They told him in no uncertain terms to forget his rendezvous! Determined to carry out his orders however, Osbourne continued. That was until Japanese bullets shattered the windscreen of his jeep and ventilated one of his lorries. He decided to turn back, smartly.

After about half a mile, he encountered Colonel Wiley and his Gurkhas. The Gurkhas were not retreating as such. They were actively seeking the enemy and enjoying it. Osbourne teamed up with them but despite their valiant joint efforts, a fighting retreat was, of course, inevitable. It was during that desperate rearguard action that Jack Osbourne met the indomitable Colonel Toosey for the first time, too.

Not only were Jack's post-war lecture notes fascinating to read, they also proved invaluable to me and I am therefore deeply indebted to June for allowing me the free use of them. June carries out invaluable work of her own, as she is currently the Welfare Officer of the Oxfordshire Yeomanry Trust.

Having met these stalwart people and seen them with Bill and Beryl, one is immediately struck by the fact that theirs is an uncommonly tight-knit fraternity. In army terms, it is not unlike that of the 'Pals' regiments of the First World War. Most regiments have a certain *esprit de corps*, but there was much more than that here. It was a kindred spirit born of the hellish adversity that thankfully, few today ever have to endure. Perhaps that is what Bill meant about having good mates around you. Few people today could ever hope to be so fortunate in their friendships. Sadly, fewer still would ever understand.

As for my late grandfather, Diddy, his treatment (or lack of it) at the hands of the Japanese ultimately cost him half of his stomach, largely due to the effects of that 'sporting torture' so beloved of the guards. In fact with Diddy, it almost became a case of 'you name a medical condition, he'd probably had it', including the dreaded tuberculosis, but somehow he survived them all, earning himself the family nickname of 'Captain Scarlet' for his apparent indestructibility.

But his was, in reality, a grim survival. All too often, he awoke sweating and screaming in the middle of the night. He still suffered the mental and the physical pain of what the Japanese had done to him.

It has since occurred to me that if I had never known the true Diddy, then neither had his own son. My father, Jim, was born in November 1937 and was just over two and a half years of age when he was evacuated to a farm in Leigh, Dorset, due to the bombing of London. By the time Diddy came home, my father hadn't seen him for five years and had reached the age of seven being raised on that Dorset farm. He often told my brother and me later, how hard it was for him to leave that farm and go 'home' to the bombed-out Bermondsey area of south London with the strange couple that were apparently his real parents. Life in a prefab was certainly different from that on the farm.

Anyone who has ever watched *The Two Ronnies* on television and laughed along with their characters, 'the two Londoners in the pub', has met Diddy. Ronnie Corbett's character looks and sounds so uncannily like him that I am certain that at some point, Mr Corbett must have seen Diddy wearing that donkey jacket and flat cap, supping a pint in a Bermondsey pub and talking in that wonderfully deadpan way even while his friend, (in this case Ronnie Barker), comically tries to prompt his memory or finish his sentences for him, seemingly un-noticed! That character is Diddy to perfection. Maybe one day I might get to thank Mr Corbett personally for creating him, or more accurately, for re-creating Diddy.

But there was always the ever-present unseen shadow of Diddy's experiences as a prisoner of the Japanese lurking in the background. After enduring everything that the Japanese could throw at him, as well as the horrible after effects of it all, the seemingly indestructible 'Captain Scarlet' was finally beaten by the deaths of every member of his immediate family. First his wife, Mary, died after suffering her third successive stroke. Shortly afterwards his daughter, Brenda, the eldest of his two children, was killed by a brain haemorrhage at the age of fifty.

As if all this wasn't enough for him to bear, Diddy died of a broken heart on 23 November 1988, two days after I broke the news to him of his son's sudden death, also from a brain haemorrhage. Jim, my father, had been just two months short of his fifty-first birthday at the time of his death. Diddy was probably wondering just what on earth he'd ever done to deserve it all.

A BRIEF HISTORY OF BILL'S REGIMENT, THE QUEEN'S OWN OXFORDSHIRE HUSSARS

Bill's regiment was one of those formed during the Napoleonic wars under the Provisional Cavalry Act. The Oxford troop was the third such troop raised under the act in 1798. At the time, the troop numbered about fifty strong and was armed with swords and pistols.

For about fifteen years after the Battle of Waterloo, the Yeomanry's chief duty was as a sort of police force, preserving peace at home. The uneasy peace after the long wars was full of trouble as the people rebelled and rioted over such issues as taxation, high prices, unemployment, bad trading conditions and anything else that seemed worthy of a riot. It was later said that the Yeomanry had stood firmly between the country and insurrection.

In 1800 it was the food riots and in 1830 it was the agricultural riots and an act of land repossession that had the Yeomanry turned out in large numbers. In 1835, it was a happier occasion; that of a royal visit by Queen Adelaide to Oxford, that had the Yeomen turned out to form a guard of honour. It was as a result of this that the Oxfordshire Yeomanry gained the title 'Queen's Own'.

In the late 1880's, the regiment still consisted of the old style foot soldier, but when they came under the command of Lord Valentia, an old officer of the 10th Hussars, they began to acquire a reputation for smartness and good horsemanship. In 1896, Edward, Prince of Wales, became the regiment's Colonel-in-Chief, an honour indeed and one that finally put the regiment on the map. In fact, it was because they were now effectively a mounted regiment that they got the undeserved nickname of 'Queer Objects on Horseback', which of course is derived from the initials of the regiment's title.

Responding to the call for volunteers, the regiment sent fifty men with horses to South Africa to help fight the Boer War, in 1899. The regiment gained a battle honour at Dreifontein in which the captain of the Banbury troop was killed. Five other members of the regiment were mentioned in dispatches.

After the Boer War, the regiment was reorganized on a 'four squadron' basis. The lessons learned on the veld were taught in earnest and regimental training was increased to fourteen days per year at camps.

The regiment went from strength to strength through the Great War. Battle honours were gained at Messines and Armentières in 1914; at Ypres in 1915; at St. Julien and Bellewaarde; at Arras, Scarpe and Cambrai in 1917 and at the Somme, St. Quentin, Lys, Hazebrouck, Amiens, Bapaume, Hindenburg Line, Canal du Nord, Selle and Sambre in 1918. In short, the regiment distinguished itself in just about every major battle fought in France and Flanders.

During the Second World War the regiment fought with distinction in France, Belgium, Holland and finally in Germany after the Normandy landings of 1944. In fact, it was men of this regiment who liberated the notorious concentration camp of Belsen.

Understandably, there are no regimental battle honours relating to the Far East. Singapore and Malaya were hardly triumphs. But perhaps there ought to be a special battle honour for the Burma-Thailand railway, which if nothing else was a dogged battle for survival. It was a battle that the men of the regiment fought with great courage and fortitude; a fact that becomes apparent when it is realized that more than a quarter of the men of the Oxfordshire Yeomanry who were captured in Singapore, died as prisoners of the Japanese.

131

The regiment itself was taken off the active list after 169 years service and disbanded in 1967, although the regimental association continues to thrive. In 1992, the association produced a private book called *Yeomanry Memories*. Issued on a strictly 'members only' basis, this hardbound book records the fascinating history of the regiment through the eyes of those who served in it. I feel privileged indeed to have been allowed to read a copy and to have had the opportunity of meeting just a few of the remarkable members of the regiment. May their stories never be forgotten.

Having researched and written this book, Bill and I have, of necessity, read it many times. What we would both now like you to do is to go back and read it again just once more; but this time, for the fallen.

BIBLIOGRAPHY

Allbury, Alfred, *Bamboo & Bushido*, Robert Hale Ltd., London, 1955

Arnold-Foster, Mark, *The World At War*, Collins, London, 1973

Clements, Patricia, *Sticky Dewi* , Blackie & Co. Ltd., London, 2001

Cosford, J.S., *Line of Lost Lives*, Gryphon Books, 1988

Nicholls, T.E., *Yeomanry Memories*, Privately printed on behalf of the Oxfordshire Yeomanry Regimental Association, 1992

Rawlings, Leo, *And The Dawn Came Up Like Thunder*, Rawlings-Chapman Publications, 1972

VIDEOTAPE

The Bridge on the River Kwai: Revealed, Channel 5 documentary programme

Seven Wonders of the Industrial Age, BBC documentary series, Episode Three: The Trans-Continental Railroad

INDEX